GRACE-GIFTS

jack parfain

19/6/83

D1522452

Michael Griffiths

GRACE-GIFTS

WILLIAM B. EERDMANS PUBLISHING COMPANY
GRAND RAPIDS, MICHIGAN

First USA edition, August 1979, by arrangement with Overseas Missionary Fellowship, Belmont, The Vine, Sevenoaks, Kent, England. The UK edition of this book was published under the title *Cinderella's Betrothal Gifts*.

Reprinted, November 1980

Library of Congress Cataloging in Publication Data

Griffiths, Michael, 1928-
  Grace - gifts.

  First published in 1978 under title: Cinderella's bethrothal gifts.
    1. Gifts, Spiritual. I. Title.
BT767.3.G74 1979   234'. 1   79-15583
ISBN 0-8028-1810-2

Contents

Introduction

How can we justify a further book on this subject? The
project was suggested at a small conference of missionary
directors working in East Asia, who were meeting in
Singapore to discuss how missionaries could become
more effective as Christian workers. When doing some
theological groundwork for this conference, I quickly
realized that what we really needed to consider was the
subject of 'spiritual gifts'. We wanted to know what
endowment by God is necessary for a church-planting
and church-perfecting ministry. Our goal was practical,
not theoretical or controversial.

If you groan mentally at yet another contribution on
this subject, my sympathy is entirely with you. The
material in this booklet was not prepared in the first
instance for publication at all, for it would seem impossible for anybody to say anything new on this subject
which has attracted so much recent attention. Inevitably
any such study must owe a great deal to other writers and
speakers, although many conclusions were arrived at from
Scripture independently. My wife, on hearing John
Stott speaking in Singapore recently, said that it sounded
as though we had been listening to each other. Actually,
the first draft of this book had already been written before
John Stott's *Baptism and Fulness* was published, and our
independent study of Scripture itself sometimes led us to
the same conclusions. Further request that the material
should be published was made at the Belgrave Heights
Convention in Australia in 1976 after an exposition of
1 Corinthians 12-14.

However, this book differs from positions adopted by
some other writers on this subject in two main particulars.

Charismata have not ceased

First, many evangelical authors who are biblical in
orientation are prepared to argue (not always convinc-
ingly) that certain 'gifts' are no longer exercised today.
Now, I am perfectly convinced that gifts of the Spirit
will no longer be needed 'when that which is perfect has
come' (one of the chief points of 1 Corinthians 13).
However, I find this solution a difficult and unhappy
one, when adopted by those who know the Bible to be
both inspired and inerrant. It would be unkind and
inaccurate to describe those who take such a dispensa-
tional view of gifts as being theologically liberal, although
they do sometimes arbitrarily snip out certain passages
of the New Testament (*e.g.*, parts of 1 Corinthians 14) as
no longer applicable today. This is an uncomfortable
position for a Christian true to the Word of God, who
would instantly repudiate the exercise of critical scissors
by people who wish, for example, to remove from the
sacred text material which they regard as mythical or as
a product of the later church.

Such a position is adopted as 'a reply to the charismatic movement' (if we may use so vague a term for the
moment). Unfortunately, as a 'reply' it is most unconvincing. People identified with the charismatic
movement merely ignore it as an unconvincing attempt
to evade what they believe to be the clear teaching of
Scripture.

The standpoint of this booklet is that our understanding of spiritual gifts must be determined directly from
Scripture itself and, if possible, by an examination of the
usage of biblical words in relation to their context. It
must not be based on dogmatic assertions drawn from
pragmatic experience. Thus I have tried to arrive at an
objective biblical understanding of what 'an apostle' is,
or what it means to 'prophesy', trying to define these in

strictly biblical terms. This seems a more helpful corrective to more extreme emphases within the charismatic movement which cause such disquiet and misgiving to some other biblical Christians. Common objections or apprehensions about certain gifts can be met, not by denying that they are still given, but rather by insisting upon a careful biblical study of what these gifts mean in the New Testament and by exercising them only in the way which Scripture itself clearly teaches. In other words, 'The Bible is a sufficient guide in all matters of faith and conduct.'

Charismata are not to be sought

Secondly, I raise a specific question as to whether the Bible really does teach that spiritual gifts should be sought by individuals. Many have assumed 'seeking' to be orthodox belief, and it certainly used to be the standard teaching among evangelical Christians long before the present interest in speaking in tongues, healing, miracles, etc., was aroused.

The teaching of 1 Corinthians 12 as a whole appears to be that we should accept the gifts sovereignly distributed by the Holy Spirit,[1] and the place in the body which the Father has sovereignly assigned to each of us.[2] Accordingly it seems probable that 1 Corinthians 12.31 is not a command to 'seek' or 'covet' gifts (an imperative), but rather a rebuke against being 'jealous' of the gifts exercised by others (an indicative). In other words, the verse should read not 'Earnestly desire . . .' but 'You earnestly desire the greater gifts. But I show you a still more excellent way.' The traditional interpretation depends upon the English translation as 'seek' or 'covet', but, as we shall see, this may not be the best understand-

[1] 1 Cor. 12.11   [2] 1 Cor. 12.18

ing of the meaning of the original words in the original context.

If this is so, then we ought not to urge people to seek any gift. Thus we may allow that all the gifts mentioned in the New Testament (and others not mentioned[3]) may be sovereignly given today if God so chooses. Whether they are or not depends *not* upon our seeking, but upon God Himself who sovereignly chooses to bestow or to withhold gifts from congregations or individuals, just as *He* pleases. Such an approach removes a great deal of heat and anxiety from the whole issue. To state it even more simply, gifts are given (as the basic meaning of the word would suggest) and not sought.

Evidence of continuing confusion

The need for further clarification concerning the charismata was brought to my attention forcibly in a recent missionary application paper. In answer to the question: 'Have you any experience of charismatic gifts?' the candidate replied simply 'No'. He was nonetheless accepted. This shows just how far negative over-reaction against contemporary attitudes can force us away from a biblical usage of words.

We frequently speak of 'pastors' and 'evangelists' although they are only mentioned once each in the New Testament lists of gifts, and yet ignore almost completely other words which have far greater prominence in the New Testament. Or again, there are people who see practically all Christian problems, even moral ones, as a result of demon possession, or who identify other gifts as being a kind of Christian clairvoyance.

Are there any biblical guidelines to help us find our way through this confusing maze? Of course there are. Very little of what follows is particularly original, and the

[3] See John Stott, *Baptism and Fulness*, page 89

various cross-references to other writers, particularly biblical commentators, will indicate how much I am in their debt. But I rejoice that, although controversy between Christians is distressing, when positively carried out in a Christian manner it may help us all to a much clearer view of what was earlier disregarded or confused, and we may discover afresh the self-authenticating character of biblical inspiration.

One thing remains to be said: the views expressed here are my own and should not be taken as representing the official position of the Overseas Missionary Fellowship as a whole. The Principles and Practice of OMF state that their missionaries 'must be prepared to have fellowship with all believers holding fundamental biblical truths, even if they differ widely in their judgment of other points of interpretation of Scripture, and on church order and government.' As far as the contents of this book are concerned, my fellow missionaries will doubtless differ widely, though I hope it will be a positive contribution to a greater mutual understanding.

—MICHAEL GRIFFITHS

Let no one look down on your youthfulness, but rather in speech, conduct, love, faith and purity, show yourself an example of those who believe.

Until I come, give attention to the public reading of Scripture, to exhortation and teaching.

Do not neglect the spiritual gift within you, which was bestowed upon you through prophetic utterance with the laying on of hands by the presbytery.

Take pains with these things; be absorbed in them, so that your progress may be evident to all.

Pay close attention to yourself and to your teaching; persevere in these things; for as you do this you will insure salvation both for yourself and for those who hear you. *(1 Timothy 4:12-16)*

(New American Standard Version)

1 What are spiritual gifts?

THERE are at least five New Testament words translated 'gifts' and four of them derive from the root *do*—meaning 'give'. While some of these words can be used generally for man's gifts to one another and to God (*e.g. dōron* occurring 19 times), most of them denote primarily the gifts that God, the 'giver of every good and perfect gift', gives to men (*dōrea* 11 times and *dorēma* twice).

Important words

However, there are two words used in the New Testament to which we must give greater attention. Both of them have the ending -*ma*, a common ending in New Testament Greek to indicate the result of an action. The additional suffix -*ta* is the plural form. Thus the word used in Ephesians 4.8 of the Ephesian 'gifts', *people* God gives for the equipment of the saints, is *domata* which occurs five times in the New Testament. We can see that this word is made up of the stem 'to give' *do-*, with the ending -*ma* to mean 'the result of giving' namely 'a gift', and with a further addition of -*ta* indicating a plural number of the results of giving, *i.e.* 'gifts'.

The commoner word is that from which we derive the currently-popular word 'charismatic', and the rather inaccurate way in which this is frequently used requires us to look again carefully at its proper biblical meaning and usage. The word *charisma* is derived directly from *charis* which means 'grace'. Thus 'the result of grace' *charis* is a spiritual gift *charis-ma*. In the plural form it is *charisma-ta* meaning the many results of grace. The relationship between grace and gifts is too obvious to be accidental, as is clear from the following key passages about gifts:

13

Romans 12.6: 'Since we have *charismata* that differ according to the *charis* given to us.'

1 Peter 4.10: 'As each has received a *charisma* employ it . . . as good stewards of the manifold *charis* of God.'

1 Corinthians 1.4,5,7: 'I thank my God always concerning you, for the *charis* of God which was given you in Christ Jesus, that in everything you were enriched in Him in all speech and all knowledge . . . so that you are not lacking in any *charisma*.'

This relationship is clear in German where spiritual gifts are called *Gnadegabe*, literally 'grace-gifts'.

It is as though the grace of God shines upon the prism of the congregation and is refracted into a spectrum of 'grace-gifts'. Gifts are not personal attributes or acquisitions, but rather outpourings of God's grace.

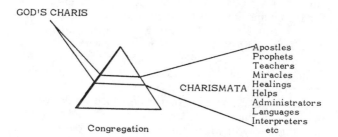

GOD'S CHARIS

CHARISMATA

Apostles
Prophets
Teachers
Miracles
Healings
Helps
Administrators
Languages
Interpreters
etc

Congregation

Charismata are the results of grace and God's grace is ministered to the congregation and manifested through spiritual gifts. Thus Goldingay defines *charisma* as

'God's grace finding particular and concrete actualisation'.[1] We notice that the origin of a charisma is not in the person who exercises it, but that it derives directly from God's grace being poured upon the congregation.

[1] John Goldingay, *The Church and the Gifts of the Spirit*, page 5

We have been so preoccupied with 'grace' in the form of God's *common grace* to all mankind and particularly His *saving grace* to all believers, that we very readily overlook this further usage of the word grace, which we might call *serving grace* or *congregational grace*.

Notice please how this concept throws much light upon other Scriptures.   Thus Paul says, 'I laboured more than them all, yet not I, but the *grace* of God which was with me'.[1]   We are told that 'with great power the apostles were giving witness of the resurrection of the Lord Jesus and abundant *grace* was upon them all',[2] and that after hands were laid upon the Seven, already men full of the Spirit and of wisdom, Stephen 'full of *grace* and power was performing great wonders and signs among the people'.[3]

All of the 17 references to *charisma*, apart from 1 Peter 4.10, occur in Paul's writings.   Its meaning is difficult to define because it is not a common word.   We can learn almost nothing from material outside the New Testament; therefore the context is virtually our only guide.[4]

It means a favour bestowed, a gift of grace, a gift freely and graciously given.   The word is used in the general sense of the free gift of salvation, in such familiar passages as Romans 5.15,16; 6.23, and of the 'gifts and calling of God' in Romans 11.29. Without accepting this *charisma*, we are not yet Christians.   In a biblical sense, someone without any experience of charismatic gifts would not be a Christian at all!   It seems wrong therefore that the word '*charismatic*' should be used to describe certain Christians, when it must properly and necessarily be the definition of every Christian.   Paul speaks of every man having 'his own gift' of marriage or celibacy;[5] he longs to see the Romans in order to impart to them some

[1] 1 Cor. 15.10   [2] Acts 4.33   [3] Acts 6.8
[4] Kittel, ix, page 403   [5] 1 Cor. 7.7

spiritual gift,[1] and remarks that the Corinthians are not lacking in any gift.[2]

The word is used for what we commonly think of as 'charismatic gifts' in Romans 12.6; 1 Corinthians 12. 4,9,28,30,31, and in the single non-Pauline reference in 1 Peter 4.10. Three further references suggest that such a gift may be bestowed through corporate prayer (2 Corinthians 1.11) or through laying on of hands (1 Timothy 4.14; 2 Timothy 1.6).

Interestingly, the word often translated 'spiritual gifts' in the opening verse of 1 Corinthians 12 (*pneumatikōn*) may not actually mean that in the context. The genitive plural of the adjective *pneumatikōn* may be neuter, meaning 'spiritual things',[3] or masculine, meaning 'spiritual persons'.[4] Here it is more probably masculine, meaning 'one who possesses the Spirit' or 'Spirit-filled people'. Thus it may be better to read this verse, as the context seems to demand, 'concerning the inspired (persons)'.

Perhaps the way in which we have tended to think of certain individuals in the church as possessing a particular spiritual gift as personal property may be a distorted emphasis. Apostles, prophets, evangelists and pastors/teachers may themselves be described as gifts (*domata*) of the ascended Christ to His saints,[5] but when we are thinking of the various edifying activities or functions exercised by individuals (*charismata*) it would be better to think of those corporately as the pouring out of God's grace upon the congregation as a whole, the manifestation of that grace being the variety of activities which we have come to describe as 'spiritual gifts'. The difference is more than merely a different emphasis: gifts are not so much possessed as exercised, and are supremely

---

[1] Romans 1.11   [2] 1 Cor. 1.7   [3] As in 1 Cor. 9.11, 14.1, 15.46
[4] As in 1 Cor. 2.15, 3.1, 14.37   [5] Ephesians 4.8

the operation of God's grace upon the congregation.

It should be noticed, incidentally, that although we tend to talk about the 'gifts of the Spirit', in Romans 12 and 1 Peter 4 God the Father is the author of spiritual gifts and in Ephesians 4 they are the gifts of the ascended Christ. Moreover, in 1 Corinthians 12.4-6 there is deliberate reference to all three Persons of the Trinity, 'the same God . . . the same Lord . . . the same Spirit'. We see then that spiritual gifts (*charismata*) are the results of the grace of God, of all three Persons of the Godhead, poured out upon the church.

2 How many gifts?

IN responding to the question 'How many different gifts are there?' John Stott replies,

'At least twenty are specified in the New Testament, and the living God who loves variety and is a generous giver may well bestow many, many more than that.'[1]

Because there are several lists which overlap partially with one another and because the same gift may be referred to under different names, we have brought the information together into one chart, which appears on pp. 20 and 21.

In the first column, we have taken the *1 Corinthians 12.28* list of eight gifts as normative because it sets the gifts in order of precedence, 'first, second, third . . .'.

In the second column, exactly the same sequence is found in the succeeding verses *1 Corinthians 12.29-32*, which list only seven gifts (omitting 'helps' and 'administrations' and adding 'interpreting').

In the third column, the *1 Corinthians 12.8-10* list is the longest, containing what some call 'The Nine Gifts of the Spirit', but only five of these gifts coincide with the first list.

In the fourth column, *Romans 12.6-8*, there is a list of seven gifts, five of which are not directly mentioned in the same words in any of the Corinthian lists.

In the fifth column, *Ephesians 4*, the brief list of five (or probably only four—see below) categories contain two new words, but we should notice that the gifts are *domata* and not *charismata*.

Peter's list of only two seems almost too short for inclusion, but he specifically uses the word *charisma* (1

[1] Op. cit. page 90

Peter 4.10), and mentions simply speaking (possibly including apostles, prophets, pastors, teachers and evangelists), and serving (presumably helps, including giving, showing mercy, administration and leadership).

The references to the five spectacular gifts which are worth nothing if exercised without love (1 Corinthians 13) and the five contributions to public worship in 1 Corinthians 14.26 give us two further parallel lists in columns 7 and 8.

For reasons explained later, it should be noticed that the 'teaching of wisdom' and 'of knowledge' are regarded as an enlargement of the gift of teaching, and that 'pastors/teachers' are also included in the same horizontal level. There is possibly some overlap between 'serving', 'giving' and 'showing mercy' in Romans and the 'helps' of Corinthians, and a probable correspondence between those 'who lead' (or preside) in Romans and the 'administrations' in Corinthians.

We can only agree with F. F. Bruce when he says concerning 1 Corinthians 12.11: 'the list is not intended to be exhaustive'.[1] A comparison of the different lists amounting to some twenty different items suggests that neither Paul nor Peter was intending to produce a single exhaustive list; each was rather illustrating what he meant when emphasizing either the variety of gifts or the unity of the purpose for which they were given.

[1] F. F. Bruce, 1 *and* 2 *Corinthians*

1 Cor.12.28	1 Cor.12.29-32	1 Cor.12.4-11	Rom.12.6-8	Eph.4.11
'God has appointed'	'all are not..'	'charismata diakonia energemata phanerōsis'	'charismata'	'domata'
3 persons & 5 functions	3 persons & 4 functions	9 functions	7 functions	4 or 5 per
(first) apostles	apostles			apostles
(second) prophets	prophets	prophecy	prophecy	prophets
(third) teachers	teachers	teaching of wisdom (logos sophias) teaching of knowledge (logos gnoseōs)	he who teaches	pastor/ teacher (poimēn)
			he who encourages	
				evangelists
		faith		
miracles	miracles	effecting of miracles		
gifts of healing	gifts of healing	gifts of healing		
helps (succourers)			service	
			he who gives	
			he who shows mercy	
administrations (steersman)			he who leads (presides)	
		discerning of Spirits		
various kinds of tongues	speaking in tongues	various kinds of tongues		
	interpret	interpretation of tongues		

...t.4.10-11 ...arisma' ...unctions	1 Cor.13.1-3 'If I have..' 5 functions	1 Cor.14.26 ' each one has a ...' 5 contributions	Persons who Manifest	Greek Noun/Verbs
...ever ...ks ...les of (logia)			Peter Paul Barnabas Silas Timothy	apostoloi
	(prophecy)	(a revelation) apokalupsis	Antioch five including Paul & Barnabas Silas Agabus Philip's daughters	prophētēs prophēteis
	all mysteries (all knowledge)	(a teaching) (didachē)	Antioch five including Paul Barnabas	didaskaloi didaskō didaskalia
		(psalm newly composed)	Barnabas	parakaleō paraklēsis
			Philip Timothy	evangelistēs
	(all faith)			pistis
			Peter Paul Stephen Philip	dunameis
			Peter Paul	charismata iamatōn
...ever ves			(The Seven)	antilēmpseis diakonia
	(give all)		Barnabas	ho metadidous
				ho eleōn
			Elders (directors)	kubernēseis ho proistamenos
			Peter Paul	diakriseis pneumatōn
	(tongues of men & angels)	(a tongue)	Paul	glōssa
		(an interpretation)	Mark	hermēneia diermēneuo

21

3 A spectrum of gifts

IT is obvious that some individuals exercise more than one gift. Reference to the ninth column reminds us that Paul and Barnabas are both listed among the 'prophets and teachers' in Antioch,[1] and yet both are shortly afterwards called 'apostles'.[2] When Barnabas first appears[3] he is exercising the gift of giving[4] while his nickname reminds us that he is a supreme example of the gift of encouragement.[5] Paul also manifested on occasion the gift of healing and miracles and apparently claimed the gift of languages. Thus each exercised at least five gifts.

Even more confusing is the fact that not only may one individual fulfil several functions, but the biblical definitions themselves merge into one another and overlap.

Rather than reading as distinct gifts:

APOSTLE PROPHET TEACHER SHEPHERD

they appear as a continuous spectrum

APOSTLEPROPHETEACHERSHEPHERD

We find this overlap when the Antioch church leaders are described as 'prophets and teachers' without saying which were which and suggesting that possibly all five were both. In Ephesians 4.11 the absence of the article before 'teachers' indicates that 'pastors/teachers' are a single group. (It is possible that the phrase 'apostles and prophets' in Ephesians 2.20 and 3.5 may be a similar type of overlap.)

Silas who, together with Timothy, was included with

---

[1] Acts 13.1   [2] Acts 14.14   [3] Acts 4.36,37
[4] Rom. 12.8   [5] Rom. 12.8

Paul as 'apostles of Christ'[1] is described as a 'prophet'[2] when he is said to 'encourage and strengthen the brethren with a lengthy message'. So a prophet, in fulfilling his ministry, exercises the gift of encouragement. Paul on two occasions describes himself as 'a preacher (herald), an apostle and a teacher'.[3]

It is true that words like prophet, teacher, encourager, pastor or evangelist each have their own distinctive shade of meaning, but both teaching and encouraging, for example, are part of the prophetic function. He is a poor evangelist who does no teaching. The effective church-founding apostle (see later) also must engage in evangelism, teaching and encouraging which are essential parts of his apostolic task.

> 'All these activities, which shade too finely into one another for rigid distinctions to be profitable or even accurate, are of an advantage to the Christian assembly . . . .'[4]

The gifts of grace appear like a spectrum; each colour may be distinguished from others as distinctively violet, blue, indigo etc. in the centre, but merges into the adjacent colours at the edges. Each gift has its own distinctive purpose, but overlaps with neighbouring gifts. No one individual displays the whole spectrum of the gifts of God's manifold grace (though Paul must have approached close to it), but one individual might possess several related gifts.

In the next section, we shall observe that apostles are always evangelizing and any biblical definition of prophecy is bound to include some aspects of teaching. It is precisely this aspect of overlapping definitions which is so confusing. However when we see them all as the results of grace, the consequences of God blessing a

---

[1] 1 Thess. 2.6   [2] Acts 15.32   [3] 1 Tim. 2.7, 2 Tim. 1.11
[4] C. K. Barrett, *A Commentary on the First Epistle to the Corinthians*, page 317

congregation, then we are not surprised that they are closer to a continuous spectrum of God's blessing than to a series of isolated activities or functions.

Remembering this, let us now look at the distinctive shades of meaning of each of the biblical words used for describing the gifts of grace.

4 The gifts distinguished

IT should again be underlined that we are trying to find out how these words are used and are to be understood within the Bible. In some cases, where a word is rare, it is impossible to be definite and therefore foolish to be dogmatic.

1 Apostles

The gift of an apostle is described as 'first' and is mentioned specifically three times, always as a personal office and not an aptitude. Confusion arises because some insist that an apostle can only be defined as one of 'the men who have accompanied us all the time that the Lord Jesus went in and out among us, beginning with the baptism of John, until the day that he was taken up from us . . . a witness with us of His resurrection'.[1] Certainly the Twelve were unique and could have no successors; their unique authority is to be found in Scripture. Scripture itself, however, does speak of others as apostles, beside Paul, namely: Barnabas,[2] Silas and Timothy,[3] Andronicus and Junia (Junia[4] is feminine!), Epaphroditus 'your apostle',[5] and the apostles of the churches.[6]

Paul's use (three times) of the verb *apostellō* is significant; in Romans 10.15 of preachers being 'sent'; in 1 Corinthians 1.17 of being 'sent to preach the Gospel', and in 2 Corinthians 12.17 of Paul's 'sending' of his own deputies. The word is wide in its usage and not restricted to a small group.

[1] Acts 1.21,22   [2] Acts 14.14   [3] 1 Thess. 2.6   [4] Rom. 16.7
[5] Phil. 2.25   [6] 2 Cor. 8.23

Goldingay points out that the word 'apostle' is 'ety-
mologically equivalent to missionary', and that 'apostles
are perhaps the pioneer missionary evangelists through
whom Christian communities are founded'.[1] This
meaning is supported by the interesting expression in 1
Corinthians 9.2, 'If to others I am not an apostle, at
least I am to you', *i.e.* as the missionary founder of the
Corinthian congregation. This can be paralleled by the
expressions 'I planted',[2] 'as a wise master-builder I laid a
foundation'[3] and 'I became your father through the
gospel'.[4] When a pioneer missionary goes to a new
tribe, they have no Bible of their own. The missionary
is initially their only source of apostolic doctrine so that,
even in this special sense, he carries apostolic authority.
It does not seem biblically necessary to deny the continuing existence of apostles in this secondary sense of
pioneer church-planting missionaries. In missionary
societies today, we need this charisma more than any
other. It is the 'first' of the gifts, and the planting of new
congregations still needs to be done cross-culturally in
many parts of the world.

On the other hand, I think there is a great danger in a
recent book which says, 'Let us watch and pray for
apostles to be raised up . . . let us recognize and submit
to them as they appear.' This doctrine is currently
taught in some of the more extreme and separatist parts
of the house-church movement, and seems quite different
from that of the New Testament, where an apostle brings
the congregation into existence. Surely only missionary
founders of new congregations could claim this kind of
secondary apostolic status. We should beware of self-
styled apostles who wish to put themselves in authority
over us and of status-seekers who divide congregations

[1] Op cit. page 11   [2] 1 Cor. 3.6   [3] 1 Cor. 3.10
[4] 1 Cor. 4.15

in order to grasp a prominence denied them both by society and responsible church discipline.

In view of the modern distrust of authority in general, it is pleasing to find in some circles a fresh recognition of proper authority in the local church. ('Obey your leaders,' we read in Hebrews 13.17.) However, because some groups seem to overstress that authority, we should notice that in the Bible there are limits even to apostolic authority. As Protestants who have shaken off the yoke of one big Pope in Rome, we must beware of exchanging him for a multitude of little local popes demanding absolute obedience and submission to their personal interpretation of Scripture or the will of God for the congregation or for individuals.

The apostles refused to obey the commands of Israel's legitimate religious leaders.[1] Paul withstood the apostles face to face when he knew them to be wrong.[2] Scripture knows nothing of infallible religious leaders.[3] Even authoritative teaching from the pulpit is not above Spirit-guided criticism.[4] Prophesying and preaching are mixed phenomena; Spirit-filled utterance may be mixed with fleshly elation, half-truth and even error: therefore both must be tested and weighed. It is a Christian duty to exercise our critical faculties, albeit with courtesy and charity. We do no Christian speaker a service by regarding his teaching as infallible.

As we have seen, Paul reminds the Corinthians of his apostolic authority; if to others he is not an apostle at least he is to them as founder of the congregation. But then he goes on to appeal to their judgement: 'I speak to intelligent men; judge what I say'.[5] Though Paul himself never uses the word 'disciple' of anybody, Timothy was certainly his protégé and 'child in the faith'; yet to him

[1] Acts 4.19,20   [2] Gal. 2.11   [3] 1 Cor. 8.2, 13.9
[4] 1 Cor. 14.29; 1 Thess. 5.21   [5] 1 Cor. 10.5

also Paul says, 'Consider what I say and the Lord will
give you understanding in all things'.¹ The Christian
therefore is to exercise his own mind and to look for the
guidance of the Lord, not merely to accept what his
spiritual father may say. The most compelling passage
of all says, 'Let each man be fully persuaded in his own
mind'.² Christian leadership never dominates other
Christians, least of all in the area of judgement where
each is answerable directly to his own Master. 'Do
not be called Rabbi; for one is your Teacher and you are
all brothers. And do not call anyone on earth Father,
for One is your Father, He who is in heaven. And do
not be called leaders; for One is your leader that is
Christ.'³

2 Prophets

Prophecy is the most commonly referred to of all the
gifts. It comes in no less than seven lists as against the
single reference each to 'pastors' and 'evangelists'. This
fact, together with the way in which prophesying seems as
common as praying in the Corinthian congregation,
should make us hesitate before committing ourselves to
the viewpoint that this gift no longer exists. Michael
Green points out how widespread prophecy was in the
New Testament churches;

> 'not only in Jerusalem and Caesaria, but in Antioch (11.
> 27; 13.1) Rome (Rom. 12.6), Corinth, Thessalonica
> (1 Thess. 5.19,20) and the churches of Asia Minor (Rev.
> 1.3). Both Luke and Matthew indicate that Jesus
> anticipated a continuation of prophecy among His
> followers (Matt. 10.41f.; Luke 11.49).'⁴

There is an underlying problem here. F. F. Bruce puts

¹ 1 Cor. 2.7   ² Rom. 14.4-5   ³ Matt. 23.8,9,10
⁴ Michael Green, *I believe in the Holy Spirit*, page 169

his finger unerringly on it when, in commenting on 1
Corinthians 14.31, he says that

> 'the ability to prophesy, at least on occasion, is open to
> most, indeed to all, members of the church, although
> only a few may exercise it at any one meeting, speaking
> one by one, so that all may learn and all be encouraged.
> In 11.4f., prophesying appears to be as common an
> exercise as praying and that on the part of men and
> women alike. . . .'[1]

Alec Motyer says

> 'Every Christian is potentially a prophet. The pouring
> out of the Spirit on all flesh carries with it this result,
> "and they shall prophesy" (Acts 2.18).'[2]

This reminds us that the words added by the New
Testament writers to the words of Joel imply that
prophecy will be a gift common to Christians,[3] and we
might also remember the comment of Moses, 'would that
all the Lord's people were prophets'.[4] Earle Ellis
comments,

> 'In several passages in Acts, the phenomenon of prophecy
> is ascribed to Christian disciples generally. . . .   Along-
> side these texts is the equally significant fact that Luke
> restricts the term or title *prophētēs*, as it is used of his
> contemporaries, to a select number of "leading men"
> (cf. Acts 15.22) who exercise considerable influence in
> the Christian community.'[5]

He then goes on to cite the group from Jerusalem visiting
Antioch including Agabus,[6] a group resident in Antioch,
including Barnabas and Paul,[7] and the two prophets who
accompanied the Jerusalem decree to Antioch, Judas
Barsabbas and Silas.[8]

Thus there does seem to be a difference between the
prophesying in which all Christians may properly engage

[1] op. cit., page 134   [2] Alec Motyer, *New Bible Dictionary*,
page 1045   [3] See Green, op. cit., page 168   [4] Num. 11.29
[5] Earle Ellis, *The Role of the Christian Prophet in Acts* ch.2:
Apostolic History and the Gospel, page 55   [6] Acts 11.27f,
cf. 21.10   [7] Acts 13   [8] Acts 15.22,23

one by one, and those who are specifically given the title
'prophets'. Nevertheless, prophesying seems to be a
common gift of all Christians which the Corinthians are
urged to develop.

To many, the very meaning of 'prophesy' in common
speech suggests foretelling the future. However, when
we examine the Acts of the Apostles, there are only three
specific instances of predictive prophecy, including
Agabus' prediction of the famine and of Paul being
bound.[1] The Corinthian believers were told that they
could all prophesy one by one; and if their prophecies
were entirely predictions of the future in every meeting,
it would have been somewhat overwhelming. It would
seem, then, that although some New Testament prophecy
told of what would happen in the future, much more was
related to the immediate situation, as indeed was a great
deal of the message of the Old Testament prophets.

Within the New Testament, we find three descriptions
of what prophecy is which, while not strictly 'definitions'
as such, certainly encourage us to feel that we are right
in believing that New Testament prophecy was only
relatively rarely connected with foretelling the future.

Acts 15.32: 'Being prophets themselves, encouraged and
strengthened the brethren with a lengthy message'
(we have already noticed that the ministry of these
prophets included the other spiritual gift of encouragement).

1 Corinthians 14.3: 'One who prophesies speaks to men
for edification and exhortation and consolation!'
and again

1 Corinthians 14.31: 'You can all prophesy one by one,
so that all may learn and all may be exhorted.'

Significantly, not one of these biblical descriptions
suggest that New Testament prophecy was *primarily*

[1] Acts 11.28, 21.10,11

predictive. Clearly *some* was (*e.g.* Agabus), addressed to a particular situation or particular individuals, and without any permanent significance or lasting application to other situations. Generally, however, its main function seems to have been encouragement and teaching for edification.

Definitions are difficult, but the following may be helpful:

'It is the gift by which God keeps his church up-to-date, able to understand and live in the changing world.'[1]

The Roman Catholic charismatic writer Stephen Clark says:

'Prophecy is the gift by which God speaks through a person a message to an individual or the whole Christian community. It is God making use of someone to tell men what He thinks about the present situation or what His intention is for the future, what He thinks that they should know or be mindful of right now. Prophecy is not necessarily for prediction of the future (although this frequently happens).'[2]

We should not ignore the view of Stott that

'the biblical understanding, dating back to Old Testament days, is that a prophet was an organ of divine revelation, to whom the Word of the Lord came, and who therefore spoke the very words of God (*e.g.* Ex. 4.12; 7.1,2; Jer. 1.49, 23.16,18,22,28). In this meaning of the term, which is the essential biblical meaning, I think we must say that there are no more prophets, for God's self-revelation was completed in Christ and in the apostolic witness to Christ, and the canon of Scripture has long since been closed.'[3]

He argues particularly that, because 'apostles and prophets', which come first and second in the Ephesian and Corinthian lists, are said to be the foundation on which the church is built,[4] once the foundation has been

[1] Goldingay, op. cit., page 7   [2] Stephen Clark, *Spiritual Gifts*, pages 18-19   [3] Stott, op. cit., page 100   [4] Eph. 2.20, 3.5

laid apostles and prophets in this sense are no longer needed. We would all surely agree that in the sense of an authoritative Word of God of equal authority with that of Scripture itself, we can understand this qualification and indeed warmly support it. He goes on to allow the possibility of 'subsidiary meanings' but, having defined a prophet as 'the mouthpiece of God', 'the organ of fresh revelation', he understandably thinks it unwise to allow the possibility of prophets today. But does 1 Corinthians 14 imply this kind of infallible prophecy?

Green adopts a different position:

> 'It was the direct word from God for the situation on hand, through the mouth of one of his people (and on occasion, this could apparently be any Christian, including those not reckoned to be "prophets").'[1]

David Pawson in a taped sermon defines prophecy as 'a word in someone's mouth which they have not prepared, an immediate inspired utterance from God'.

It can be seen immediately that, if this position were allowed to suggest that any believer might produce a prophecy which was considered to carry authority equivalent to that of the written Word of God itself, there could be very real dangers to the church.

The safeguard here is that Scripture itself commands that prophecy must always be tested carefully;[2] when a prophet has spoken, the rest should then 'judge' or 'weigh' what has been said.[3] This suggests that prophecy, like preaching, is a mixed phenomenon. We have all had the experience when preaching of finding ourselves saying something we have never ourselves until that moment seen so clearly or been able to express so simply, and which had not come into our original preparation. There is always this supernatural element which we

---

[1] Green, op. cit., page 170   [2] 1 Thess. 5.20,21
[3] 1 Cor. 14.29

would immediately ascribe to the assistance and indeed the 'utterance' of the Spirit. In the same message, however, we may, either at the time or in retrospect, wish that we had not said certain things or expressed ourselves in a certain way for fear of misunderstanding, or giving offence, etc. We are only too well aware that this was carnal and not of God.

The very fact that prophesying is *not* to be regarded as automatically authoritative but is to be carefully weighed suggests that the kind of prophecy referred to in 1 Corinthians 14 cannot be regarded as in the same class at all as the direct words of God through the Old Testament prophets.

It is for this reason that I am unhappy with the emphasis or custom which decrees that what purports to be 'prophecy' must always be delivered in the first person as the direct words of God to the congregation or to an individual. And this, for three reasons:

(i) Though the Old Testament prophets certainly used the first person, they prefaced their words with 'Thus says the Lord'.

(ii) The Old Testament prophets show a tremendous variety in their styles; compare for example the book of Malachi, where most of the verses are the direct words of God to His people, and the book of Jonah where the actual message to Nineveh is only half a verse (Jonah 3.4). Or compare Zechariah with his remarkable visions and Hosea with his down-to-earth application from his own unhappy marital experience. Why insist that prophecy must fall into a stereotyped mould when it does not in the Bible? Stereotype is more indicative of imitation than inspiration.

(iii) The very fact that the New Testament itself insists that prophecy must be tested carefully and weighed; it would seem disrespectful to do this to what has been cast in the form of an infallible direct word of the Lord.

Yet it would be even more disrespectful not to obey what
we know to be the written Word of God, commanding
us to test what may be no more than the words of man.

It is not clear what form this judging or weighing
should take. Should this be done on the spot? Or does
it mean that, because all preaching and prophecy are
mixed phenomena, our critical faculties enlightened by
the Holy Spirit will inevitably be fully active? In that
case, those things which are clearly in accordance with
God's word will carry their own self-authenticating
confirmation to our hearts; whereas that which is distorted, one-sided or positively erroneous will cause
immediate doubt in our minds and subsequent reflection
will lead to rejection of it as divine truth. Nobody may
claim as 'a prophet' immunity from the same degree of
spiritual criticism as is rightly anticipated by any preacher. The responsibility would be frightening. If our
speaking was to be regarded as infallible, the consequences
for the church who accepts as 'gospel' every word of its
minister would be alarming to contemplate.

Ellis very helpfully suggests that:

> Certain functions of the Christian *prophētēs* are clearly
> reminiscent of the role of the prophet in the Old Testa-
> ment . . . the prediction of future events (Acts 11.28,
> 20.23,25, 27.22), the declaration of divine judgments
> (Acts 13.11, 28.25-28) and the employment of symbolic
> actions (Acts 21.11). The prophets in Acts also expound
> the Scriptures and "exhort" and "strengthen" the
> disciples.'[1]

He goes on to point out that the interpretation of
Scripture, usually in the synagogues, is a key feature of
the mission of the prophets Paul, Barnabas and Silas, as
well as of Peter and other Christian leaders. It may or
may not be significant that these prophets also teach.
He goes on:

[1] Ellis, op. cit., page 56

'The interpretation of Scripture as an activity of a prophet
was not unknown in the first century since it was explicitly
ascribed to Daniel (9.2,24). It may be inferred also
from other Old Testament texts in which the prophet
uses and reapplies old biblical phraseology and ideas. . . .
The rabbis, moreover, regarded themselves, as the
teachers of Israel, to be the successors of the prophets:
they sat "in Moses' seat".'[1]

He suggests that

'It is probable that not only the miracle-working context
but also the manner of Jesus' exposition of Scripture in
the synagogue contributed to the conviction that he was
a prophet. And it could do so because such exposition
was regarded as the proper activity of a prophet.'[2]

Ellis sums up by saying, 'the interpretation of Scripture
was indeed regarded, under certain conditions, as a
prophetic activity'. And his footnote quotes Selwyn on
1 Peter: 'in the case of Christian prophets . . . the
searching of the Scriptures . . . was an important part
of their task.'

We notice that Paul's predictive prophecy[3] about the
Jews and Gentiles is largely exposition of existing Old
Testament prophecy.

The list of contributions which members may make
(1 Corinthians 14.26) includes a revelation (*apokalupsis*)
and Paul speaks elsewhere of such revelations given to
him.[4] In this Paul's experience would seem to reflect the
final book of the New Testament which we know as
Revelation, part of the permanent revelation given to us
in Scripture.

The word generally means to uncover, disclose or
unveil. We may understand it of the disclosure involved
in exposition, the exposing of some biblical truth. Paul
prayed 'that the God of our Lord Jesus Christ, the Father

---

[1] Ellis, op. cit., page 58   [2] Ibid, page 51   [3] Acts 28.25-28
[4] Gal. 1.12, 2.2; also 1 Cor. 11.23 and, significantly, 2 Cor. 12.1

of glory may give you a spirit of wisdom and revelation
in the knowledge of Him'.[1] We ought not to narrow
'revelation' to mean a vision: it includes all that we might
call 'dis-covery', *i.e.* fresh understanding and uncovering
of the meaning of the Word of God.

It can include visions and dreams, especially in primitive communities who do not yet have the Word of God.
A Bible study on dreams is worth pursuing, and will
reveal, among genuine messages from the Lord in dreams,
that some may arise from busyness[2] and that there are
false dreams.[3] In view of the danger of limelight-
seekers offering sensational dreams as a status symbol,
it is refreshing to hear from Bishop Festo Kivengere that
in the East Africa revival, the leaders might suggest that
a man's dream meant that he had eaten too much for
supper last night! The same cautious testing and careful
weighing is needed for visions and dreams as for other
purported prophecy before they can be regarded as
genuine, especially in view of biblical warnings about
divination.[4] If such spectacular revelations seem to
supplant 'Christ and Him crucified' as the centre of our
faith, we shall be justifiably cautious before accepting
them as coming from God.

It does seem permissible, then, from the discussion
above, for us to distinguish the general prophesying in
which all the congregation, both men and women, may
engage, from the ministry of those who are endowed
specifically with 'gifts' and are themselves 'gifts' given by
God to His people, set apart as 'prophets' and 'prophetesses'. There seems no biblical reason for denying that
both of these usages of the word are still valid today,
providing we do not give them the value equivalent to the
canonical biblical prophets. If there is any contradiction

---

[1] Eph. 1.17   [2] Eccl. 5.3,7   [3] Jer. 23.25-32
[4] Jer. 27.9, 29.8,9

then the Word of God in Scripture is always to be preferred.

It may be objected that the result of this analysis is to suggest that prophecy is almost no more than another word for inspired preaching and teaching. However, as has been pointed out in our treatment of the whole concept of the spectrum of grace, it cannot be denied from the descriptions given earlier that prophecy does overlap very considerably with preaching, teaching and encouragement. If Scripture itself describes prophecy in this way, then we must be cautious about pressing an understanding of the word which relies more on its English derivation than on Scriptural usage.

Again, when one considers the need of missionary work today, there is constant need for encouraging and strengthening Christians in the face of persecution and of showing authoritatively the relevance of the Word of God to existing situations. Just as much today as in that first church in Antioch, we desperately need 'prophets and teachers' in our missionary ranks.

3 Teachers

The gift of teaching, overlapping with prophecy and encouragement, is the primary means of edifying the church and building up the body. It is one of the most exciting gifts and the one with the greatest possibilities in the missionary scene today. If you really want to be stretched as a teacher, then a fascinating variety of opportunities awaits you in missionary service. Get rid of that mental image of the tedious transfer of information from the notes of the lecturer to the notes of the students without passing through the minds of either! Don't think of teaching as imparting information to people so that they can retain it long enough to pass examinations! Christian teaching has much more exciting dimensions.

The great commission contains two words for teaching.[1] The first word is usually translated 'make disciples', or, in other words, teaching with a view to commitment. Secondly, those baptized disciples are then to be taught to obey everything which Jesus commanded. Teaching that produces *commitment* is to be followed by teaching which produces *behavioural change*. Traditionally too much Christian teaching is pulpit soliloquy and nobody ever checks up to see whether anybody takes any notice or whether the teaching produces any action. Traditional theological education has been almost entirely content-orientated; increasing quantities of information have to be absorbed and subsequently regurgitated for examination purposes by students living in monastic communities. Will they be able to 'teach' in the New Testament sense? For even the most cursory examination of the letters written to the first Christian congregations show that teaching was concerned not only that Christians should *know* but also that they should *do* and *be*.

It is not surprising that the gift of teaching is included in almost every list of gifts. The ministry of Jesus Himself was a teaching ministry, and Acts refers constantly to the apostles' teaching.[2] Barnabas first started teaching the new group in Antioch on his own, but soon went to fetch Paul to help him and they taught for a year.[3] One teacher became two teachers and soon became five teachers;[4] the two first teachers are then released for missionary service, but when they come back 'Paul and Barnabas stayed in Antioch teaching and preaching *with many others* also the Word of the Lord'.[5] This constant multiplication and increase in the number of teachers is

[1] Matt. 28.19,20   [2] Acts 2.42, 4.2,18, 5.21,25,28,42
[3] Acts 11.26   [4] Acts 13.1
[5] Acts 15.35

so different from the static 'one teacher school' pattern of so many congregations.

After the controversy as to whether apostles and prophets are foundational gifts, no longer required in the churches, it is somewhat of a relief to find that nobody has any problems about the continuing necessity of teachers.

'The teaching of wisdom' and 'the teaching of knowledge'

The word *logos* may be used to mean 'preaching' or 'teaching' (as well as 'word') as in the familiar passage 1 Corinthians 1.17,18 where, literally, 'the word of the cross' equals 'the preaching of the cross'. Here is another illustration of the way in which a familiar English translation has tended to influence popular understanding of these gifts as a kind of Christian clairvoyance. If the translation from the beginning had been 'the teaching of wisdom' (rather than 'word of wisdom') this misunderstanding might have been avoided. In other modern translations, it is translated 'preaching' or 'speaking'. The placing of these two gifts at the beginning of the 1 Corinthians 12.4-11 list, which has no other reference to teaching, suggests that this interpretation is the correct one. Thus Stephen Clark writes:

'The first two gifts which St Paul mentions are teaching gifts: *the utterance of wisdom* (sometimes translated "the word of wisdom" and *the utterance of knowledge* (sometimes translated "the word of knowledge"). They are special inspirations by which God works through one person to give understanding to another person or to a group of people. A person who is given an utterance of wisdom or an utterance of knowledge can then give a lesson (an instruction or an explanation) in the Christian assembly (1 Cor. 14.26) or perhaps a special word of advice or instruction to a particular person. The New Testament in great part, especially the epistles, is made up of utterance of wisdom and knowledge, inspired

teaching. . . .   The utterance of knowledge on the other
hand, is more what we would call doctrinal teaching. . . .
St Paul, when he was speaking about the utterance of
knowledge, almost certainly does not mean a special
knowledge of facts that a person could not have known
otherwise.'[1]

This I think underlines Peter's instruction in the context
of *charisma* 'whoever speaks, let him speak as it were the
utterance of God'.[2]   We sometimes talk as though
teaching somehow required less of the Holy Spirit's help
than prophecy, as when we criticise someone for thinking
that 'prophecy is no more than teaching'.   It should be
emphasised that, in New Testament thinking, *all* Christian speaking depends upon utterance given by the Holy
Spirit.

Barrett says:

'It is not clear how (or indeed whether) a word of wisdom
and a word of knowledge are to be distinguished.'[3]

Some argue that wisdom has a practical character in the
Old Testament whereas knowledge may be speculative,
so that the first represents a practical discourse, mainly
ethical instruction, and the second an exposition of
Christian doctrine.   Barrett points out, however, that in
1 Corinthians itself knowledge is connected with practical
matters (*e.g.* 8.10ff.) and some kinds of wisdom can be
speculative.   He suggests that Paul is varying his speech
by using a parallelism, as he does earlier with 'gifts',
'ministries' and 'operations' (verse 4).   Thus one must be
cautious about being too dogmatic in distinguishing
wisdom and knowledge.

There is no reason in the text, either, to assume that
these utterances should be made spontaneously, without
preparation and study.   The Holy Spirit can illumine us

[1] Clark, op. cit., pages 9-11   [2] 1 Peter 4.11
[3] Barrett, op. cit., page 285

to come to a deeper understanding of what we study and there is much in Paul's writings, and even in the teaching of the Lord Jesus, to suggest that they are Spirit-filled utterances based upon previous Old Testament meditation.

Bridge and Phypers point out the problems of accepting the interpretation that these gifts refer to

'. . . uttering an inspired wise saying in some sort of church meeting which involves a problem or points the way forward in a hitherto intractable situation . . . once it is accepted that *any* individual Christian may give infallible, detailed guidance to a church or other Christian group, the door is opened to all sorts of problems and difficulties.'[1]

They also point out the danger that if a group of Christians are engaged in a

'take-over bid for control . . . a "word of wisdom" might seek to reverse carefully thought-out policies of the existing leadership. If the "word of wisdom" is then followed, some degree of leadership will thereafter almost inevitably lie in the one credited with the inspired gift. . . . If the "inspired word" is not obeyed, then the leadership can be denounced as "unspiritual" and a new call to the membership for loyalty and obedience will often result in division.'[2]

To sum up, then, it seems unwise to insist arbitrarily on experiential grounds that 'a word of wisdom' *must* mean what *we* say it means. It seems safer to compare Scripture with Scripture in seeking to establish the meaning of words from biblical usage and to include these two categories in that section of the spectrum of grace which we call teaching.

4 Pastors

As we have seen, the absence of the article before

[1] D. Bridge and D. Phypers, *Spiritual Gifts and the Church*, page 48-49   [2] Ibid, page 50

'teachers' in Ephesians 4.11 suggests that 'pastors/ teachers' are a single group.[1] This is the only reference in the New Testament to a pastor or a shepherd being a spiritual gift (*domata*).

Most of the biblical references to this word (*poimēn*) are either to literal shepherds or to Jesus Himself as the great shepherd.[2] However, the use of the verb (*poimainō*) make shepherding the responsibility of the *apostle* Peter[3] and Peter himself teaches *elders* to shepherd the flock,[4] while Paul similarly instructs the Ephesian *elders*.[5]

We may therefore explain the solitary reference to the pastoral gift in combination with the gift of teaching, because it is a general function of the local church elder. While on the subject of ministry in the local church, we should notice that the office of *deacon* corresponds with *helps, service, giving and showing mercy* while both *overseers* and *elders* could be described as *administrations* or *those who lead* or preside. The combination pastor/ teacher suggests that, in the local congregation, a pastor would be a teaching elder.

5 He who encourages

This gift is mentioned only once specifically in Romans 12.8. The word *parakaleō* is often translated 'comfort' in the Authorised Version. Comfort originally meant 'to make strong' but has become weakened to mean 'express sympathy'. The original idea was that of 'help' and in the books of the Greek Old Testament has the rich meaning 'that kind of comfort and consolation in distress which keeps a man on his feet when, left to himself, he would collapse. It is the comfort which will enable a man to pass the breaking point and not to

[1] See Kittel, vi page 497   [2] Heb. 13.20; 1 Pet. 2.35
[3] John 21.16   [4] 1 Pet. 5.2   [5] Acts 20.28

break.'[1] In Greek law it implies advocating and defending, and we find the cognate noun (*paraklētos*) in John 16.7-11 referring to the Holy Spirit as Comforter and in 1 John 2.1 referring to the Lord Jesus Himself as Advocate. In classical Greek, the verb is used repeatedly of encouraging and strengthening soldiers and sailors with a pep-talk before they go into battle.

Joseph of Cyprus is the outstanding exponent of this gift, nicknamed as he was *Barnabas* 'the son of encouragement' (*paraklēsis*). The Hebraic expression 'son of' suggests that it was particularly his character to encourage. Having been sent to Antioch, he immediately 'began to *encourage* them all with resolute heart to remain true to the Lord',[2] and after he and Paul had made many disciples in Galatia, they returned to Lystra, Iconium and Antioch 'strengthening the souls of the disciples, encouraging them to continue in the faith and saying "through many tribulations we must enter the kingdom of God" '.[3] Here the idea of encouragement before battle is obvious. Paul uses this word repeatedly of the ministry of helping young Christians.[4]

This would seem a spiritual gift essential to the church planter who is encouraging congregations to become independent of the missionary, particularly when preparing Christians to face spiritual battle and persecution. We have already noticed the overlap of this particular gift with prophecy.

6 Evangelists

This gift is also mentioned only once (*domata*),[5] although Philip is referred to as 'the evangelist',[6] presumably to distinguish him from Philip the apostle, and Timothy is

[1] William Barclay, *New Testament Words:* SCM 1964, page 222
[2] Acts 11.23   [3] Acts 14.22   [4] e.g. 1 Thess. 2.11, 3.2, 4.1, 5.11,14   [5] Eph. 4.11   [6] Acts 21.8

commanded to do the work of an evangelist.[1]   We may
link the 'evangelist' with the 'herald' or 'preacher' of the
Gospel (e.g. 1 Timothy 2.7; 2 Timothy 1.11 where Paul
uses the word 'preacher' together with 'apostle' and
'teacher' to describe himself).   John Stott quotes Alan
Richardson as saying that the work of the herald 'is the
telling of news to people who had not heard it before',[2]
which is what we called evangelism.   The 'evangel' was
not merely good news, but specifically good news about
the king authoritatively proclaimed by a herald.

The reason why this spiritual gift is not more frequently
mentioned is presumably because it was necessarily
exercised by the church-planting apostles, as a study of
the verb 'to evangelise' in Acts makes clear.   The verb
is used fifteen times in Acts and twenty times in Paul's
epistles.   Some significant uses are of Philip the evangelist's ministry,[3] the ministry of Paul and Barnabas[4] and
subsequently Paul's European mission.[5]   The use of the
verb supports the suggestion that this ministry was
particularly one which an apostle must necessarily exercise and is thus a further classic example of the overlap
of spiritual gifts: apostles need to be evangelists.

However, it is not confined to them, for Philip was also
an evangelist and there are two other references to the
evangelism of Christians in general.   Thus, when the
great persecution arose about Stephen, we are specifically
told that 'except the apostles' they were all scattered
abroad and went about 'evangelising'.[6]   Also, in con-
nection with this same persecution, 'some of them, men
of Cyprus and Cyrene, came to Antioch and began
speaking to the Greeks also preaching (evangelising) the
Lord Jesus'.[7]

[1] 2 Tim. 4.5   [2] John Stott, *The Preacher's Portrait*, page 30
[3] Acts 8.5,12,25,35,40   [4] Acts 13.32, 14.7,21, 15.35
[5] Acts 16.10, 17.18.   [6] Acts 8.1,4
[7] Acts 11.20

The ability authoritatively to declare the royal good news of Jesus who calls us to His kingdom and glory is not just the adoption of successful techniques to bring people to a decision, but is specifically a gift of the ascended King of the Church.[1] If good evangelists are rare enough in Western countries, the challenge is even greater in missionary situations, where church-planting missionaries need to be able to evangelise effectively in another language, making the Gospel relevant to another culture. We need to pray that God will give more national evangelists to churches throughout the world, including those who may be effective on radio and television as well as in evangelistic meetings of varying sizes.

7 Faith

This is mentioned only in the 1 Corinthians 12.4-11 list and again in the following chapter 'if I had all faith so as to remove mountains but do not have love, I am nothing'.[2] The reference to this gift in 1 Corinthians 12 is in the immediate context of the gift of healings and the effecting of miracles, and we may thus see a similar principle of overlap operating here, since both healing and miracles require a particular exercise of faith. We see that Elijah on Mount Carmel[3] manifested a remarkable faith that the Lord would choose to vindicate Himself and demonstrate His power in contrast to the weakness of the prophets of Baal.

However, we should be cautious here not to identify 'faith' either with a kind of brash presumption ('every single non-Christian who attends will be converted at tonight's meeting') or the kind of subjective hunch that someone is going to be healed which, when unfulfilled,

[1] Eph. 4.8   [2] 1 Cor. 13.2   [3] 1 Kings 18

is blamed upon the unbelief of those praying or, even more cruelly, on the lack of faith of the person for whom healing is requested.   Faith does not mean that we can 'twist the arm' of the Lord.

Can we find any further guidance in Scripture itself as to what 'faith to remove mountains' might mean?   In Matthew 17.20, the lack of faith to move mountains is the reason for the failure of the disciples to cast demons out of a boy.   In Mark 11.21-25, in the context of the cursing of the fig-tree, there is the further reference to a mountain-moving faith being exercised in prayer accompanied with forgiving others.   In Luke 17.3-6, mulberry tree-moving faith is required to go on forgiving a brother who sins against you and asks for forgiveness seven times a day.

Thus, although the biblical evidence is scanty, we should notice that, in addition to requiring such faith for exorcism, it is required more generally in 'believing prayer' and especially in order to go on believing all things'[1] in forgiving those who continue to sin against us. The mention of faith in the list of gifts of grace at least reminds us that one of the results of the outpouring of God's grace upon a congregation will be an expression of faith to perform mighty exploits for God's glory, just as Elijah did in Israel.

8 Gifts of healing

Gifts of healing are referred to in all three Corinthian lists, always together with the gift of miracles.   Miracles of healing are recorded in Acts by Peter[2] and apparently more widely in Jerusalem.[3]   Peter healed the paralysed Aeneas[4] while Paul healed a lame man at Lystra,[5] and

[1] 1 Cor. 13.7   [2] Acts 3.6ff   [3] Acts 4.30, 5.12   [4] Acts 9.33
[5] Acts 14.10

there were apparently many healings in Ephesus.[1]   Again the father of Publius was healed of fever and dysentery,[2] followed by other healings in Malta.   These healings were not confined to the healing of Christians.   No specific healing of leprosy or restoring sight to the blind is mentioned in Acts.

Some false emphases about healing suggest that obedient Christians ought never to be sick.   But in New Testament times, miracles of healing do not seem to have been available in the form of a kind of first century Health Service, such that any Christian falling ill might automatically have expected to be healed.   If this had been so, we might expect to find no record of Christians ever being sick, except perhaps as a divine chastening or punishment.[3]   This is not the case, however.   Timothy is told to use wine for medicinal purposes ('for the sake of your stomach and your frequent ailments', 1 Timothy 5.23).   Epaphroditus was sick to the point of death, but God had mercy on him,[4] and on another occasion Paul says that he left Trophimus 'sick at Miletus'.[5]   Paul also speaks of his own 'weaknesses',[6] and this may also be implied in earlier references to 'despairing of life' and being 'afflicted in every way'.[7]

Michael Green gives us some robust commonsense when he writes:

'God does not always choose to heal us physically, and perhaps it is as well that he does not.   How people would rush to Christianity (and for all the wrong motives) if it carried with it automatic exemption from sickness! What a nonsense it would make of Christian virtues like longsuffering, patience and endurance if instant wholeness were available for all the Christian sick!   What

---

[1] Acts 19.11,12   [2] Acts 28.8,9
[3] 1 Cor. 11.30   [4] Phil. 2.27
[5] 2 Tim. 4.20   [6] 2 Cor. 12.7-10
[7] 2 Cor. 1.8,9, 4.8-12, 11.24-27

a wrong impression it would give of salvation if physical wholeness were perfectly realised on earth while spiritual wholeness were partly reserved for heaven! What a very curious thing it would be if God were to decree death for all His children while not allowing illness for any of them!'.[1]

A very full and fine treatment of this subject may be found in *Miraculous Healing* by Henry Frost, the first Home Director of the China Inland Mission in North America, which is now out of print.[2]

In New Testament times, there were miracles of healing on some occasions and there were other times when Christians were permitted to fall sick and inevitably to die. So today there are still situations when miraculous healing may be experienced. While God in His common grace has granted us medical means for the curing of an increasing number of diseases, there are still many conditions which medicine cannot cure or situations, particularly in remote missionary areas, where medical means may not be available. On such occasions, Christians are always free prayerfully to seek the miraculous intervention of God's grace, while recognising that, as in New Testament times, our sovereign God has equal right to decree either health or ill-health for his children.

Many of the references to signs and wonders may include miracles of healing, even when they are not specified; but we will now consider those miracles which were not 'gifts of healing'.

9 Miracles

The miracles performed in Acts would not seem to include any 'nature miracles' like the plagues in Egypt or the Lord Jesus stilling the storm or feeding the multitude (unless we regard Philip as miraculously levi-

[1] Green, op. cit., page 176   [2] Evangelical Press, London 1972

tated to Azotus in Acts 8.39,40).[1]   However, Paul speaks
of God as one who 'supplies you with the Spirit and
works miracles among you',[2] while the writer to the
Hebrews says 'God also bearing witness with them, both
by signs and wonders and by various miracles and gifts
of the Holy Spirit according to His own will'.[3]   We know
that such miracles were performed in Jerusalem after
Pentecost[4] and that the Lord granted such gifts.[5]

Such miracles appear to be of at least four kinds:

(i) *Miracles of Judgment:* The deaths of Ananias and
Sapphira (Acts 5.5,10) and the blindness of Elymas
(Acts 13.11) would be solemn examples.

(ii) *Raising of the Dead:* Peter raised the dead Tabitha at
Joppa (Acts 9.40) and Paul later appears to have
raised Eutychus at Troas (Acts 20.10).   It should
be noted that these two apostles are only recorded
to have performed the miracle of raising the dead
once each in a life time.

(iii) *Miracles of Deliverance:* On three occasions apostles
were miraculously liberated from prison, twice by an
angel of the Lord (Acts 5.19, 12.7) and once by an
earthquake (Acts 16.26).

(iv) *Miracles of Exorcism:* Of the Seven, both Stephen
and Philip performed great wonders and signs (Acts
6.8 and 8.6), some of them being healings and some
exorcisms (Acts 8.7).   Later Paul and Barnabas
performed signs and wonders in Iconium (Acts 14.3),
and on his second missionary journey Paul cast out
the evil spirit of clairvoyance from the slave girl
(Acts 16.16-18).

It might be helpful at this point to make some remarks
about demon possession.   It sometimes becomes fashion-

---

[1] See Green, op. cit., page 178   [2] Gal. 3.5   [3] Heb. 2.4
[4] Acts 2.43   [5] Acts 5.12

able to regard practically everyone as being demon possessed, including people who may have the temerity to disagree with our interpretation of Scripture! It is therefore particularly helpful to make a biblical survey of the symptoms of demon possession found in the New Testament and the various conditions which result from it.

We find that the words *demon* (21 times), *evil spirits* (six times) and *unclean spirits* (25 times) are used almost interchangeably with each other about the same evil spirit, and it does not seem possible to draw any distinction between them.

Such demons or unclean spirits are seen in the New Testament as responsible for dumbness,[1] blindness,[2] and a woman being bent double.[3] Other symptoms are often violent, including crying out and convulsions,[4] foaming at the mouth and grinding teeth,[5] or casting oneself upon the ground or into fire or water.[6]

This suggests that demon possession is evidenced by clear outward symptoms causing either deafness, dumbness, blindness or some other physical complaint, or obvious violent bodily actions and cries. There do not seem to be instances of people being quietly or discreetly demon-possessed!

It should also be noticed that in the New Testament individuals are not permitted to blame their sins upon diminished responsibility due to demon possession. Thus Jesus says that 'out of the heart of man, proceed the evil thoughts and fornications, thefts, murders, adulteries, deeds of coveting and wickedness, as well as deceit, sensuality, envy, slander, pride and foolishness. All these evil things proceed from within and defile the man'.[7]

[1] Matt. 9.32, 12.22; Mk. 9.17; Lk. 11.14   [2] Matt. 12.22
[3] Lk. 13.11   [4] Mk. 1.23, 3.11
[5] Lk. 11.39   [6] Matt. 17.15; Lk. 4.35, 9.38-43 etc.
[7] Mk. 7.21-23

James says that 'each one is tempted when he is carried away and enticed by his own lust'.[1] We should not therefore blame upon the devil or upon demons things which Scripture itself attributes to the world and the flesh.

To the vexed question of whether a Christian may be demon-possessed, one can only reply:

(i) that there is no record of this happening to a Christian in the New Testament;

(ii) that the expression 'what harmony has Christ with Belial' and the whole idea of a Christian being 'the temple of the living God'[2] is against it happening.

(iii) Luke 11.24-26 speaks of the unclean spirit finding the 'house' empty, and bringing back seven others so that the last state is worse than the first. The immediate context is the power of Jesus to overcome 'the strong man' and to throw him out. Once the Lord Jesus is in possession, who will bind and overpower Him?

This is not to deny that a Christian may be demon-oppressed and exposed to demonic attack, but to say that a Christian could be demon-possessed would imply that the Lord is powerless. It would suggest that the Holy Spirit can be driven out of His temple by evil spirits. This appears theologically unacceptable.

We should notice that the reference in Hebrews 2.4 suggests that signs, wonders, miracles and gifts are a particular confirmation of the apostolic testimony to the words of the Lord Jesus, while Paul tells the Corinthians that 'the signs of a true apostle were performed among you with all perseverance, by signs and wonders and miracles'.[3] Quite a strong case could be made, particularly if one associates miracles with signs to attest

[1] James 1.14   [2] 2 Cor. 6.15,16   [3] 2 Cor. 12.12

the ministry of the original apostles, to say that the gift
has ceased.   In the four categories of miracles above
Luke seems deliberately to select examples to authenticate
the apostolic ministries of both Peter and Paul.   Certainly in Scripture as a whole the working of miracles in the
Old Testament seems to have been concentrated in
certain periods of history, such as the Exodus and the
time of Elijah and Elisha, and it could equally be argued
that we might anticipate that the ministry of the Lord
Jesus and the confirming of the apostolic testimony might
be such a period.   We have also noted the comparative
rarity of the apostolic miracles of raising the dead and the
complete absence from Acts of specific references to the
healing of leprosy or the giving of sight to the blind
(except for Paul's temporary blindness).

But whilst recognising the relative infrequency of
miracles, we should still surely keep our minds open to
the possibility of such miracles today, particularly perhaps in primitive pioneer situations, where there is a need
for some confirmatory witness of the apostolic testimony.
While stories from Timor in Indonesia, for example, have
undoubtedly been exaggerated by sensationalists, it does
seem that some miraculous intervention of God was truly
experienced.

I must also say, however, that I have known missionaries in particularly difficult and unresponsive areas
who prayed specifically to be given the gift of miracles.
I personally have never known that prayer answered in
the affirmative.   The expectation of one missionary had
been that the performance of a miracle would have made
a deep impression and brought people pouring into the
churches.   An interesting object lesson took place shortly
afterwards in the same area; evangelistic meetings
conducted by a well-known Japanese evangelist were
very well attended.   A couple of months later, a further
series of meetings was advertised by another group who

imitated very closely the pattern of posters and leaflets used for the earlier campaign. These advertised the performance of miracles 'rapidly one after the other' and people were invited to come and see this remarkable display. Attendance at these meetings was very small indeed: only a very small number compared with the ordinary evangelistic meetings which had taken place earlier! Modern sophisticated people are particularly afraid of being taken in by ingenious illusionists, with the result that the sceptical did not even bother to attend, leaving merely the curious who (in the absence of any report of remarkable conversions) were presumably little more than temporarily entertained.

10 Gifts of service

Helps (antilēmpseis) is mentioned only once, in 1 Corinthians 12.28. It is a rare word not used elsewhere in canonical Scripture although the verbal form is found in Acts 20.35 'You must *help* the weak' and also in Luke 1.53,54 'He has filled the hungry with good things; and sent away the rich empty-handed, He has given *help* to Israel His servant'. It is also used in 2 Maccabees 8.19 for help in battle, and seems to imply succouring the needy.

If the idea is basically that of helping the poor, weak and sick, then this is the kind of work for which the Seven were first appointed in Jerusalem, helping to provide for the physical needs of the widows and serving at table.[1] However, Bittlinger says that, according to a recently-discovered papyrus, this was a technical word in the field of banking and refers to the administration of money. If this is so, it suggests helping the poor by almsgiving and corresponds with two of the gifts in the Romans list 'he who gives' and 'he who shows mercy'. If we follow

[1] Acts 6.1,2

this usage, we may have a more direct reference to those whose ministry it is to take care of church accounts and particularly the distribution of funds to the needy.

It would seem proper to associate this gift with the *serving* (*diakōnia*) mentioned by Peter, the three gifts mentioned in Romans 12, and also the allusion in 1 Corinthians 13.3 (literally) 'if I turn all my property into morsels of food'. Direct biblical references to these gifts are scanty, however, and they do not seem to have attracted the same attention as other more spectacular gifts in recent writing.

It seems important to insist that such practical helps are also *charismata* and that the work of organizers, treasurers, typists, houseparents, hostesses, etc. is thoroughly biblical and requires apportionment of the Holy Spirit just as much as speaking gifts. Paul compares the importance of such quiet and discreet members to the human organs of reproduction, modestly concealed, but at least as important as the organs of hearing or seeing.[1] It is good to remember this when attending a large meeting. At first sight, it looks as though the speaker is doing most of the work. Actually an extraordinary number of people are serving the Lord: a planning committee organised it; a secretary wrote letters. Others made arrangements. Somebody else designed the programme. Someone else arranged music. Somebody cleaned the hall. Somebody else lit the boiler. Others arranged the chairs and flowers, microphones and other paraphernalia. A whole team of people have been cooking and preparing food and are now ready to serve it. Other people welcome visitors, give out hymn books, show people to their places and sell books. If the speaker ever had to do it all on his own, he would soon realise what a small amount of the work done has been

[1] 1 Cor. 12.22-26

his! What a large number of people are required to cooperate effectively together to produce a really good meeting. It is more simple if it is just a chairman-introduces-the-speaker-who-then-speaks-Amen kind of meeting; but a really interesting meeting with a variety of presentations of differing kinds, will involve still more people in careful planning, rehearsing and preparation of material.

Admittedly the first three gifts are placed in some kind of order of importance but these other gifts are equally 'gifts of grace' and we require the grace of God in order to fulfil them adequately.

11 Administrations

Earlier this year, I was travelling on a Greek airline and idly scanned the instruction book to passengers; I was arrested by the words 'ho kubernētēs kai tō plērōma'. I recognised two biblical words and wondered why the airlines should write about 'the steersman and the fullness . . .'. Reference to the more easily-understood English instructions revealed that 'the captain and the crew' welcomed me aboard. The word for administrations (*kubernēseis*) is derived from the word *kubernētēs*, used in modern Greek for a pilot or a captain and in the New Testament also for a ship's captain[1] or a steersman.[2] Just as the helmsman steers or pilots the ship, so those with 'gifts of direction' should guide the progress of a congregation. This spiritual gift should be possessed and exercised by church elders, bishops, moderators and by the directors of evangelical societies. The same word is also used in the Greek Old Testament[3] of 'counsellors', where Kittel suggests the best translation would be 'clever direction'.

[1] Rev. 18.17   [2] Acts 27.11   [3] Prov. 1.5, 11.14, 24.6

The music 'Sailing the Seas Depends Upon the Helmsman' is currently popular in Mainland China. The importance of the helmsman increases in a time of storm and it is ironical that in Acts 27.41 the ship ends up on the rocks! This spiritual gift is of great importance at times of difficulty and crisis, and often such times help to develop and cultivate the gift even more. (Hornblower may be read with profit as an apt illustration of the man who is always thinking ahead and directing the course of the ship!)

This gift appears to be related to the gift of leading or presiding referred to in Romans 12.8 and 1 Thessalonians 5.12 (*proistamenoi*) generally used in the vernacular of that time for 'officers'. It does seem appropriate that in the chart we should put 'administrations' and 'leading' on the same horizontal level.

It is interesting to notice the variety of words used for church leaders in the New Testament. In Acts, following the elders of the Jews we get elders of the church in Jerusalem and again in the churches of Galatia. In Romans, we get this word for 'the one who presides' (*proistamenoi*) and in Corinthians 'administrations' (*kubernēseis*). In Philippians we get overseers and deacons while Colossians has no particular word. Thessalonians repeat the 'one who presides' and the pastoral epistles give us overseers, elders and deacons. The letter to the Hebrews introduces another word for leaders (*hegoumenoi*) which occurs three times. In view of this interesting variety in the New Testament congregations, it is remarkable that as Christians we have been prone to be quite so dogmatic about 'the proper New Testament church order'!

We should ponder the significance of the fact that Scripture puts teaching gifts at the beginning of the list, whereas we tend to put our administrators first. Are we sometimes in danger of copying worldly and secular forms of administration? This ought to encourage directors and other administrators to have a proper humility towards and to honour fellow-workers who exercise apostolic-church-planting, teaching and prophetic functions.

On the other hand so many churches become programme-orientated and lose sight of their goals: they seem to have little sense of progress or direction. Administration therefore is an essential gift: we need steersmen to direct us.

12 The gift of discernment

This gift is referred to only once,[1] immediately before the reference to different kinds of languages and the interpretation of languages. The need for this gift has already been indicated in 1 Corinthians 12.1-3, reminding Gentile Christians with a pagan background that before they were converted they had been 'moved' to speak by evil spirits associated with idol worship. The danger of false prophets, spurious tongues or even a deliberate misleading of Christians by evil spirits counterfeiting genuine communication makes this gift of great importance.

Illustrations in the New Testament include Peter with Ananias and Sapphira;[2] Peter again with Simon Magus;[3] Paul exposing Bar-Jesus[4] and Paul discerning that the pious (albeit factually correct) words uttered by the slave girl sprang from an evil spirit.[5] The similar reference in 1 John 4. 1 reminds us of the importance of discerning whether messages brought to us in the church are from men, from Satan or truly from God Himself. This gift helps us to identify whimsy and subjective fancies

---

[1] 1 Cor. 12.10   [2] Acts 5.3   [3] Acts 8.20   [4] Acts 13.10
[5] Acts 16.17

dressed up as visions or revelations, fanaticism, errors, cynicism or other distortions of Christian truth.

We have already seen the need to 'test everything carefully' and to 'weigh' what is said.

David Watson[1] says:

> 'The tests are clear:
> (a) Is Jesus Lord of that person's life? "No one can say 'Jesus is Lord' except by the Holy Spirit" (1 Corinthians 12.3).
> (b) Is Jesus Christ acknowledged as Perfect Man and Perfect God? "By this you know the spirit of God: every Spirit which confesses that Jesus Christ has come in the flesh is of God" (1 John 4.2).
> (c) Is there a measure of true godliness and holiness about the person? "Every sound tree bears good fruit, but the bad tree bears evil fruit. . . . Thus you will know them by their fruits" (Matthew 7.15-20; cf. 2 Peter 2).'

The placing of this in a list of 'gifts of grace' reminds us of the importance of being able to discern the difference between the real and the spurious. The more objective tests given above are important but, as David Watson goes on to say, 'there can be a spiritual ability, given by the Spirit, to distinguish between the spirits'. Not all Christians are equally able to discern between that which is real and that which is counterfeit. Bishop Festo Kivengere quotes an aged African lady who after a long, loud and uncharitable harangue remarked quietly, 'I did not see the mark of the crucified hands in what you said!' Then there is always the danger of the person who wants to get on the bandwagon and be one of the in-group. It is an old problem in a new guise: to distinguish between the brother who has something to say (from the Lord) and the brother who has to say something (so as not to be left out).

[1] David Watson, *One in the Spirit*, page 92

Discernment has to be a genuine spiritual gift of God's grace. It is true that some Christians are naive and gullible and eager for that which is sensational; but it is also true that others of us are cautious, conservative and critical. The gift of discernment is not necessarily to be identified with the latter group! It requires a God-given ability to discern that which is good and real and wholesome, true, abiding and God-glorifying. Every congregation and gathering of Christians needs warm, spiritual, respected brethren who will exercise this function in the body.

13 Speaking in languages

Reference to the chart will show that this gift is referred to in all five of the Corinthian lists but, interestingly enough, in none of the others. How are we to understand this word *glōssa*? Does it mean that when we speak in 'tongues', we speak to God in prayer? That is certainly a possible understanding of it. Or could it mean that if you speak in your 'mother-tongue', which may be incomprehensible to the rest of the congregation, that you are certainly understood by God who understands all languages, but you only edify yourself because nobody else understands what you are saying? I suspect that many readers have already made up their minds about this, although there may be some who are still uncertain. We may simply accept that we have here biblical warrant for 'speaking in tongues', which is a perfectly possible interpretation; but there is much to be gained from thinking carefully through the total biblical teaching again.

> 'The noun *glōssa* has only two known meanings, namely the organ in the mouth and a language.'[1]

A cardinal rule in biblical interpretation is that identical

[1] Stott, *Baptism and Fullness*, page 112

expressions have identical meaning, so there is strong
linguistic presumption that the 'languages' referred to in
Acts 2.4-11 has the same meaning also in 1 Corinthians
12-14. After all, if on the day of Pentecost Jerusalem
was full of people speaking many languages, then it is not
too far-fetched to expect that in a large cosmopolitan
seaport city like Corinth, you would not infrequently
have overseas visitors: Parthians, Medes, Elamites,
dwellers in Mesopotamia, Judea and Cappodocia, Pontus
and Asia, Phrygia and Pamphylia, Egypt, districts of
Libya around Cyrene, Cretans and Arabians and visitors
from Rome. In such a multi-lingual port, there must
have been many occasions when someone wanted to
speak in their own language, which would be incomprehensible to the predominantly Greek-speaking congregation.

It must be remembered that my original examination
of 'gifts' related to the qualifications and the training of
contemporary missionaries. Nowadays, before accepting somebody as a missionary, we give them a Modern
Language Aptitude Test to get a rough idea of whether
they have any natural aptitude for languages. (Interestingly, this does not necessarily have anything to do with
intelligence quotients but it does give a useful rough
guide for steering missionary candidates away from
countries with more difficult languages to those which
possibly have easier ones, or even rejecting some people
altogether. If this makes you unhappy, please see the
later section on the relationship between natural talents
and spiritual gifts.) No missionary discussion today can
overlook the fact that an essential component in a
missionary's usefulness is going to be his ability to speak
one or more languages. For the first term of missionary
service, the time involved in learning a language and the
restrictions of inadequate language will be a major factor.
In several countries people really need to learn two new

languages! Any missionary society constantly wrestles
with this problem of communication.

Conversational English is certainly understood by
better-educated people in most large cities today, but
even so, only the other day I came head on into collision
with the problem of language. I was invited to preach
to a Hokkien-speaking congregation in Taiwan: but the
church had nobody available who reckoned that he
could translate my English into Hokkien. The matter
was finally settled by my preaching in Japanese and being
interpreted directly into Hokkien.

But if the problem exists in the modern world, it seems
unrealistic to suppose that it never occurred at all in the
Ancient World. We often seem to assume very readily
that everybody in the Mediterranean world could speak
and understand Greek, just as British tourists today seem
to believe that everybody in the world can understand
English if you speak it loudly enough! We know that
Paul and Barnabas hit this problem at Lystra, where they
spoke the Lycaonian language.[1] The existence of this
problem in the Corinthian context is clear when Paul
says 'if then I do not know the meaning of the language,
I shall be to the one who speaks a barbarian and the one
who speaks will be a barbarian to me'.[2] The word is
onomatopoeic, 'barbarian' being a derogatory term for
non-Greek-speaking people whose language therefore
sounded like *bar-bar*. Just as many missionary travellers
today, when invited to address a congregation, are
inevitably faced with the question 'who will interpret?',
it is surely apparent that such a problem must also have
occurred from time to time in the emerging congregations
of the first century.

Should people be allowed to contribute in unfamiliar
languages? Everything Paul says is explicable in terms

[1] Acts 14.11-14   [2] 1 Cor. 14.11

of regulating this problem, and we ought not to reject
this explanation out of hand and dismiss it perfunctorily
as 'anti-charismatic'. It is a view held by many sincere
Christians and you will find it lucidly argued by Stott.[1]
Neither does this explanation deny the possibility of a
'charisma'. People who do not speak a language are
always impressed by another's apparent fluency and
readily call it 'a gift for language'. Anybody who
regularly has to preach in a recently-acquired language
recognises how much he needs the grace gift from the
Holy Spirit to speak effectively. It is an essential gift
for taking the Gospel to all nations!

I think, if we are honest, we shall see that both under-
standings raise problems as we go through the text (some
of them partly due to translation), and certainly I have
no wish to be dogmatic or to cause division. Love is our
aim, and we must live in peace together and therefore
respect one another's right to adopt either of these two
possible interpretations, or indeed others.

Both Green[2] and Goldingay[3] do not hesitate to accept
the view that private language-speaking is definitely
biblical, and while others may have no personal experience of this ourselves, we are impressed by the manifest
reality of the experience of others, evidenced by real and
lasting blessing in their lives.

Goldingay gives three functions of speaking in tongues:

'1. For the individual, it can be a sign that his conversion
is real, a testimony to him and to others that something
has happened to him (Acts 10.45ff., 11.15-18). The
language used may not be intelligible to anyone present,
but that does not matter, since it is the fact of the experience, the medium rather than the message, that
constitutes the sign.

[1] Stott, op. cit., pages 112f   [2] Green, op. cit., pages 161f
[3] Goldingay, op. cit., pages 7f

The sign-value of tongues must not be over-stressed, however (cf. 14.22); 'a sign' easily becomes 'the sign'. Without actually mentioning tongues, the Sermon on the Mount warns against thinking that the exercise of a gift is the proof of being a Christian (let alone an evidence of spirituality) (Matthew 7.21ff., cf. Luke 10.20).

2. For the individual in his subsequent Christian living, tongues can be a way of 'praying in the Spirit' that he will find a great value . . . (see below for Goldingay's Scriptural justification of this).

3. Tongues can also be used in ministry to other people, the means of a message in heavenly language coming direct from God to them. . . . It may only be used when accompanied by the exercise, by the same person or someone else, of the ability to interpret tongues. . . .'[1]

Goldingay continues

'Paul, then, is essentially negative in his evaluation of tongues in relation to the congregation. But he makes it clear that this does not mean total rejection of the gift. "Thank God I am more gifted in ecstatic utterance than any of you" he says, and "I should be pleased for you all to use the tongues of ecstasy" (vv. 18, 5a); we should not try to explain away these expressions of appreciation. Paul in fact makes clear why he places a certain value on tongues.

1. Tongues really is a way of "talking with God" (v. 2) . . . . While the fact that words cannot be understood by men is a reason for playing down the use of the gift in public, this fact is less of a disadvantage when the gift is used in private, for God, to whom prayer or praise in tongues is addressed, can understand them.

2. Tongues really "is good for" (RSV edifies) "the speaker" (v. 4). . . . Tongues thus seems to fulfil a function not unanalogous with that of art or music for some. . . .

3. Tongues . . . is not a higher, but a lower form of prayer (v. 14)—but it is a real form of prayer. It is

[1] Goldingay, op. cit., pages 7-8

neither the key to holiness nor the peak of spiritual
achievement (as the Corinthians show)—but it may be
a valuable feature of elementary and basic Christian
experience, a real blessing from God at that level.'[1]

It should, however, be strongly emphasised that 'all
do not speak with tongues',[2] and it is quite arbitrary to
divide Christians into two classes of 'haves' and 'have
nots' in relation to this gift. Please consider carefully
the implications of the final section of this booklet,
discussing the real meaning of 'seeking' and 'desiring
earnestly' in relation to gifts in general (therefore also
to 'tongues'). It should also be remembered that the
Corinthian letter with its encouragement to 'be zealous
for spiritual gifts' is addressed to the congregation as a
whole. It should not therefore be used to encourage
every Christian to believe that he ought to manifest all
the gifts, or any one of them in particular.

Note:

More attention should be given to the admittedly difficult
verse 1 Corinthians 14.21 in its context: 'In the Law it is
written, "By men of strange tongues and by the lips of
strangers I will speak to this people, and even so they
will not listen to Me," says the Lord.' Michael Green is
very clear in expounding the reference to Isaiah 28.11,12:
'Indeed, He will speak to this people through stammering
lips and a foreign tongue, He who said to them, "Here is
a rest, give rest to the weary," and, "Here is repose," but
they would not listen.'
He says:

'The point is that Israel spurned the message of the
prophets, delivered as it was in clear unambiguous
speech. And so God, by way of punishment had to
speak to them through the strange, unwelcome tongues
of the Assyrians. These tongues came to them because

[1] Ibid. pages 21,22   [2] 1 Cor. 12.30

they were "unbelieving". They did not believe what the prophets had said, and they did not obey. The tongues of the Assyrians were, therefore, "a sign to those who did not believe".'[1]

Palmer Robertson is also very interesting:

'It is quite striking to note the similarity of contexts in Isaiah and in Paul. Isaiah's problem was the childish nation of Israel; Paul's problem is the childish church of Corinth. By setting his remarks in a context comparable to that of Isaiah, Paul reinforces the weight of his words. The Corinthians indirectly are admonished not to stumble into the same error as Israel of old. . . . It is not that Paul simply snatches up an isolated aphorism to apply to his circumstances. He knew full well that tongues in Isaiah appeared as a sign of covenantal curse. . . . How did tongues serve as a sign of covenantal judgment for Israel? In a very literal sense, the "tongues" of Pentecost represented the taking of the kingdom away from Israel and the giving of the kingdom of men of all nations. . . . No longer will God funnel his gracious work of salvation through a single nation. Instead, God now shall speak all languages to all the peoples of the earth.'[2]

On this understanding, the 'languages' of Acts 2 served as 'a sign' which communicated to unbelievers.[3] God has not assigned the gift of tongues for the up-building of the believer but as a particular sign of judgment on Israel which brought blessing to all the nations in a multitude of languages. The expression then 'tongues are for a sign' is seen as an explicit reference to Pentecost which was a sign to unbelieving Israel and explains the apparent confusing conflict between verse 22 where tongues are for unbelievers and verse 23 where unbelievers react unfavourably to languages.

[1] Green, op. cit., page 165   [2] Palmer Robertson, *Tongues: Sign of Covenantal Curse and Blessing*, pages 46-48
[3] 1 Cor. 14.22

14 Interpretation of tongues

This gift is referred to in three lists and always in association with the gift of languages, as might be expected.

In the worship of the synagogue, there was always an interpreter who, when the Scriptures were read in Ancient Hebrew, would translate them into contemporary Aramaic. Jews were familiar with the need for an interpreter. Interestingly, Aaron is described as Moses' interpreter and Papias refers to Mark as the 'interpreter' of Peter. This usage of the word strengthens the case for *glōssa* being translated as (foreign) 'languages'.

The word is used in Luke 24.27 of Jesus 'explaining the things concerning himself', and also in John 1.38,42, 9.7 and Acts 9.36 with the ordinary meaning of 'translated'. This would seem to contradict the extraordinary assertion that an interpreter of 'tongues' need not understand the 'language' himself, but is speaking out the word which God gives him. The natural meaning of 'translate' in its general biblical usage seems to imply that the interpreter must have a direct understanding. It is always easy to discover whether there is somebody present who speaks Japanese or Cantonese beforehand and, if there is no interpreter, to keep silent. If no name can be given to a language, then it is not possible to know until afterwards whether it can be 'interpreted' or not, and this makes it more difficult to obey the biblical injunction. Frankly, to follow one speech incomprehensible to the congregation with a further explanation of general meaning from someone who also finds it incomprehensible and is speaking by direct illumination does not seem to me to be a fair understanding of this passage.

Some writers suggest that tongues plus interpretation are the equivalent of prophecy but, if this is so, it is rather difficult to understand why 1 Corinthians 14 should have been written to demonstrate the superiority of prophecy. It could, I suppose, be argued by those of

us who have had to tolerate long hours of listening to
something being interpreted into two languages that
direct speech is much more profitable, because there is
no attenuation of meaning and one can say so much
more in the time.

Let us remember again that the understanding of the
word as 'translation' still involves a spiritual gift. Those
of us who listen frequently to translated messages or who
have to be interpreted ourselves are very clear that a
gifted interpreter manifests the unction of the Spirit just
as much or even more than the speaker whom he interprets.
There can be no doubt that the plain meaning 'interpreter'
(of one known language into another) requires the grace
of God to do it effectively to the blessing of the congregation.

5 How may we receive these gifts?

IN making initial notes for this section, I immediately scribbled down words like 'sovereignty' and 'seeking', but when I started looking at the biblical verses, I came up with several other answers. Eventually, I found I had seriously to qualify our commonly-accepted understanding of what 'seeking' or 'desiring' gifts really means. Perhaps to regain the biblical emphasis we should first reread the words of the passage from 1 Timothy 4.12-16 which head this booklet.

1 Sovereignty

A free *gift* is a sovereign gift of grace given by God Himself. These gifts are particular ways in which God's grace is actualised for the congregation.

Gifts already given

The main New Testament passages on spiritual gifts all emphasise that every Christian has been sovereignly given some specific function within the body. Every one is a member of the body, and every member has a function to fulfil:

> 'as God has allotted to *each* . . . we, who are many, are one body in Christ, and individually members one of another. And since we have gifts that differ . . .' (Romans 12.3-6).
> 'to *each one* is given the manifestation of the Spirit for the common good . . . but one and the same Spirit works all these things, distributing to *each one* individually just as He wills' (1 Corinthians 12.7-11).
> 'but to *each one* of us grace was given according to the measure of Christ's gift . . .' (Ephesians 4.7).

Leon Morris says

> '. . . the local ministry could be exercised only because its
> members also possessed a *charisma*. The New Testa-
> ment does not envisage any ministry as carried out apart
> from God's good gift.
>
> It is also to be borne in mind that all church members
> had a "ministry" of some sort. "The manifestation of
> the Spirit is given to every man" (1 Corinthians 12.7)
> says Paul as he proceeds to the subject of ministering,
> and other references make it quite plain that this is no
> idle expression. Thus when he is giving directions for
> public worship the same writer can say, "when ye come
> together, every one of you hath a psalm, hath a doc-
> trine . . .".'[1]

The stress of the New Testament is that every Christian
already possesses some spiritual gift, which has been
sovereignly given to him or her. This is surely a basic
understanding and needs to be reasserted at a time when
much of our emphasis has shifted to saying that we should
'seek earnestly' for spiritual gifts. Whether this is a
correct biblical understanding, we shall consider in the
final section of this chapter.

Natural and Spiritual gifts

How do such *charismata* relate to natural gifts and
attitudes? We know that God's sovereignty means that
there are 'good works, which God prepared beforehand,
that we should walk in them'.[2] The Lord shaped
Jeremiah for his ministry, saying to him, 'before I formed
you in the womb I knew you, and before you were born I
consecrated you';[3] John the Baptist was 'filled with the
Holy Spirit while yet in his mother's womb';[4] the apostle

[1] Leon Morris, *Ministers of God*, page 62   [2] Eph. 2.10
[3] Jer. 1.5   [4] Luke 1.15

Paul spoke of Him 'who had set me apart, even from my mother's womb, and called me through His grace'.[1]

In view of all this, there seems no reason why the Lord our Creator should not give to His servants natural aptitudes which would subsequently become enriched by spiritual gifts. While we must agree that we cannot succeed in spiritual work merely by relying upon natural aptitudes, the sovereign God may well give to His servants from their mother's womb natural abilities which, when surrendered, sanctified and transfigured by spiritual blessings, can be effectively used to God's glory.

The above was written before I had had the opportunity of seeing the magnificent section in Stott's book[2] where he makes a very strong point that the Lord is both God of Creation and of Redemption. The God who chose us before the foundation of the world (Ephesians 1.4,5) and who prepared beforehand good works for us to walk in (Ephesians 2.10) is also the God of Redemption who pours His grace upon us and endues us with spiritual gifts (Ephesians 4.7,11).

> 'In view of what has been written above about the God of nature and of grace, is it not *a priori* unlikely that God will give a spiritual gift of teaching to a believer who in preconversion days could not teach for toffee, or a spiritual gift of encouragement to a brother or sister who by temperament is unsympathetic and unfriendly? It would not be impossible to God. But would it not be more in harmony with the God of the Bible, whose plans are eternal, to suppose that his spiritual gifts dovetail with his natural endowments? And that (for example) a "son of encouragement" such as Barnabas (Acts 4.36) who exercises his particular ministry both by generous giving (v. 37) and by personal friendship (e.g. Acts 9.26,27, 11.25,26), was already that kind of person, at least potentially, by creation?

[1] Gal. 1.15   [2] Stott, op. cit., pages 90-94

In this case we must look for the peculiarities of the spiritual gift of teaching and encouragement in the heightening, the intensification, the "Christianising" of a natural endowment already present, or at least latent. Thus a man may be a gifted teacher before his conversion, and may after it be given the *charisma* of teaching to enable him to expound with insight, clarity and relevance. . . .'[1]

Does this not accord with spiritual commonsense? If a man has a chaotically untidy mind by nature and cannot organise itself, let alone anybody else, it would seem a little unwise of us to entrust to him the steering of the congregation in anticipation that the Lord will give to him the gift of 'administrations'.

God has been sovereignly at work in all our lives from the earliest beginnings. We therefore see both our initial genetic constitution and our subsequent spiritual endowments as sovereignly given and perfectly fitted together.

2 Laying on of hands by Church Leaders

One of the unexpected results of my Bible study was to discover that the *charismata* required by the church might be bestowed through the laying on of hands. The Giver is always God in His sovereignty, but the channel would seem to be the properly-designated leaders of the local church. Let us look at the two crucial passages.

'Do not neglect the *charisma* within you, which was bestowed upon you through prophetic utterance with a laying on of hands by the presbytery. Take pains with these things; be absorbed in them, so that your progress may be evident to all. Pay close attention to yourself and your teaching; persevere in these things' (1 Timothy 4.14-16).

[1] Stott, op. cit., pages 93,94

Notice the stress upon working at your gift, not neglecting it, taking pains, paying close attention and persevering. But notice chiefly the relationship between the *charisma* and the laying on of hands.   I am not of course, suggesting a crude *ex opere operato* automatic giving of spiritual gifts apart from divine grace.   But does this not clearly suggest that the normal and proper channel for the giving of spiritual gifts for exercise within the local church ought to be the laying on of hands by the leaders of that local church?

> 'I remind you to kindle afresh the *charisma*, which is in you through the laying on of my hands' (2 Timothy 1.6).

It is not clear whether this refers to the same occasion as the earlier letter, so that Paul, together with the elders in Lystra, laid hands on Timothy in the situation described in Acts 16.2-3.   The similarity of the two expressions would certainly suggest that it is the same occasion, though not necessarily so.

Hands were laid upon the Seven when they were appointed.   They were already men 'full of the Spirit and of wisdom'[1] and had been selected because of that, but hands were nevertheless laid on them,[2] and both Stephen and Philip subsequently manifested spiritual gifts in their effective ministries,[3] so much so that they did much more than serve tables.   The writer to the Hebrews[4] assumes that the doctrine of laying on of hands is elementary teaching.   Should we therefore give more attention to laying hands on missionaries and Christian leaders when they are appointed, praying specifically that they should then be granted the *charismata* which they need to fulfil their tasks—as church-planting apostles, as teachers and pastors or as wise steersmen directing the course of congregations or other area of Christian work?

---

[1] Acts 6.3   [2] Acts 6.3   [3] Acts 6.8,10,15   7.2ff,55f 8.6,7,12,29,35,40   [4] Hebrews 6.2

Leon Morris, contrasting early church ministry with today's more institutional ministry, comments that

'. . . their ministry was exercised as the result of a special divine gift (*charisma*) and not of any human commissioning'.[1]

It does, however, seem possible to understand these two references in the pastoral epistles in such a way as to reconcile these two viewpoints. Decency and order within the church requires that it be the congregation which seeks God's blessing and the granting of spiritual gifts upon those whom it commissions as leaders, or sends out as missionaries. Many of us missionaries are sent out with laying on of hands, and we need to kindle afresh the *charisma* sovereignly given to us by the great Giver at that time.

This raises the interesting question of exactly *when* spiritual gifts are imparted which, strangely enough, is a question not often asked. We do not need to insist that spiritual gifts are sovereignly imparted once for all at the time of the new birth, although doubtless this is partly true. These two verses in the pastoral epistles encourage us to believe that *charismata* may be given within the church where they are to be exercised. It may also be correct to see a gift more as part of the manifestation of the grace of God given to the whole congregation and less as a personally possessed piece of property.

3 Prayer and ministry

Because the previous section suggests that *charisma* may be given through the laying on of hands by apostles and elders, this does not mean that it is necessarily restricted to this channel. The love of God is flooded into our hearts through His Holy Spirit,[2] and His blessings are

---

[1] Morris, op. cit., page 62   [2] Rom. 5.5

never restricted to narrow channels. There are other verses which suggest that *charismata* may be given through other means, for example:

> (i) 'For I long to see you in order that I may impart some *charisma* to you that you may be established; that is, that I may be encouraged together with you while among you, each of us by the other's faith, both yours and mine' (Romans 1.11-12).

This suggests that another channel of blessing is mutual ministry between fellow-believers; it is interesting to notice, incidentally, that the verb for establishing or strengthening is related to that used to describe the prophetic ministry of Silas and Judas Barsabbas in Acts 15.32.

The ministry of God's Word is thus a channel through which God's gifts of grace are mediated to us.

> (ii) 'You also join in helping us through your prayers, that thanks may be given by many persons on our behalf for the *charisma* bestowed upon us through the prayers of many' (2 Corinthians 1.11).

It could be said here that *charisma* refers to the more general idea of 'favour' rather than to the more limited idea of 'gift of grace'. But the association of prayer with the laying on of hands, as in the setting apart of the Seven[1] and of Barnabas and Paul,[2] suggests that prayer is such a 'means of grace'. Prayer for missionaries should surely be encouraged by this verse, reminding us that we should pray not just in a general sense for the blessing of missionaries, but also specifically that they should manifest those particular *charismata* which they require for an effective ministry.

4 Cultivation and development

In my original preparation this section was headed

[1] Acts 6.6   [2] Acts 13.3

'seeking' and came second only to 'sovereignty', and it is true that in many English versions this would seem to be a scriptural emphasis. Three verses immediately come to mind:

>   (i) 'earnestly desire the greater gifts' (1 Corinthians 12.31);
>   (ii) 'pursue love, yet desire earnestly spiritual gifts, but especially that you may prophesy' (1 Corinthians 14.1).
>   (iii) 'therefore, my brethren, desire earnestly to prophesy, and do not forbid to speak in tongues' (1 Corinthians 14.39).

As was suggested in the introduction, there is a problem of how to understand 1 Corinthians 12.31. Some[1] maintain that it is hardly likely that Paul would encourage the Corinthians to strive selfishly for the greatest gifts after he had just admonished them to be content with the gifts sovereignly distributed by the Spirit and the role in the body sovereignly given by God. He therefore suggests that verse 31 should be translated 'You earnestly desire the greater gifts' rather than 'Earnestly desire the greater gifts' and sees it as a rebuke rather than an exhortation. In other words Paul is saying 'you must not be jealous of the higher gifts. You must not strive after them, so let me show you a better way.'

This difficulty has been hinted at by some commentators who remark that Christians are told not to covet anything belonging to their neighbours, but it is all right for them to covet their neighbour's gifts! However this seems to run directly contrary to the whole teaching of 1 Corinthians 12.14-18, which urges them to accept the role which God has given to them and not to waste time wishing that they were exercising some different role. Feet should not try to become hands! This interpreta-

---

[1] e.g. Gerhard Iber, quoted by Bittlinger, op. cit.

tion is strengthened by the fact that the first negative
thing said about love[1] is that love is not jealous (*zēloi*)
where the relationship with 'being zealous (*zēloute*) for
charismata' is very obvious.   Earlier[2] the evidence that
they are still carnal is that 'there is jealousy and strife
among you'.   It would seem probable, then, that the
force of this verse is to tell us that we should *not* seek or
covet gifts which we do not possess.

1 Corinthians 14.1 'Desire earnestly spiritual gifts' is
not here *charismata* but *pneumatika* which may therefore
be more generally translated spiritual things.

All three of these verses, however, raise the question
of how we should translate the verb *zēloō* which is commonly translated 'seek', 'desire' or 'covet' in English
versions.   This has influenced our theology to the extent
that many of us think this means waiting passively for
gifts to be given or earnestly praying for them to be given.
It may be, however, that this verb conveys a different idea.
It is obviously the root from which words like 'zealous'
and 'jealous' are derived.   It is used generally of being
zealous for God, and particularly of the hostile attitude
of the Jews towards Christian preaching, which led to
hostile action.   Kittel[3] suggests that it means 'a human
emotion which leads to action . . . to strive after something, the consistent and zealous orientation of action to
a moral ideal'.   It is not just a passive hoping to receive,
but rather 'a striving kindled by and directed towards
these gifts'.   The use of the same root in other passages
seems relevant here: we find 'zealous for good deeds'[4]
and 'if you prove zealous for what is good'.[5]   We should
speak very firmly to anyone waiting and praying for good
deeds.   Go and do them, get out and practise them, we
should say.   The word means exerting oneself earnestly,

---

[1] 1 Cor. 13.4   [2] 1 Cor. 3.3   [3] Kittel, ii, page 886f
[4] Titus 2.14   [5] 1 Peter 3.13

striving after something, exerting effort to cultivate or develop.

This suggests that being 'zealous for *charismata*' means enthusiastic hard work to develop a gift already given, rather than merely praying to receive a gift one does not have, all perfected in a neat package. This seems to be a crucial understanding and one that is born out by other passages, *e.g.* the two passages we have considered in Paul's letter to Timothy: 'discipline yourself . . . we labour and strive . . . give attention . . . do not neglect that *charisma* within you . . . take pains with these things, be absorbed in them so that your progress may be evident to all. Pay close attention to yourself and to your teaching; persevere . . .',[1] and again 'I remind you to kindle afresh the *charisma* . . .'.[2]

Having said this of the individual's responsibility to develop his or her own gift, we must also recognise the assembly's responsibilities to encourage its members to develop their own gifts. The 'shipmaster' elder must surely give opportunity for the crew members to develop their spiritual gifts and God-given aptitudes.

The New Testament does not assume that such gifts are given only to men. We have been assuming all along that 'brethren'[3] has included the female members of the congregation. The expression 'each one'[4] 'all prophesy one by one'[5] makes no distinction of sex. Paul had earlier said that women may prophesy as well as pray, provided their heads are covered.[6] We find in the New Testament a female apostle, Junia,[7] prophetesses,[8] a female deaconess[9] and women fellow workers.[10] Unfortunately the word elders (*presbuteroi*) always occurs in

---

[1] 1 Tim. 4.7-17   [2] 2 Tim. 1.6   [3] 1 Cor. 12.1   14.6,20,26,39
[4] 1 Cor. 14.26   [5] 1 Cor. 14.31
[6] 1 Cor. 11.5; see the fascinating article by W. H. Martin in *Apostolic History and the Gospel*, p. 231
[7] Rom. 16.7   [8] Acts 21.9   [9] Rom. 16.1   [10] Phil. 4.3

the plural, so it is not clear whether this word, like brethren (*adelphoi*) is also intended to include women. Certainly 1 Timothy 3.1-13 seems to be giving instructions to leaders in the church and mentions overseers (v. 1ff.), deacons (v. 8ff.), women (v. 11) and deacons again (vv. 12,13). It certainly smacks of male chauvinism gratuitously to suggest that these women were wives rather than leaders. Many of us may question whether a woman should ever be ordained as the one omnicompetent leader, general factotum, pastor and teacher of a congregation. But then many of us are not happy to see one man exercising that kind of one-man band ministry either! Philip Crowe comments:

> 'Any vestigial concept of the clergyman as the one well-educated omnicompetent father-figure of a small static community is about as relevant to modern urban society as the appendix is to the digestive system.'[1]

If it is a question of a team ministry, a group of Christian workers serving together within a congregation, then there seems little difficulty in some members of that group being women. May I make a plea that women should not be relegated solely to making tea and preparing meals, but that real efforts be made to help women to develop their spiritual gifts: and, having developed and cultivated those gifts, to give them the opportunity to exercise them!

[1] Philip Crowe, *Ministry in the Local Church*, page 9

Conclusion

THIS study of 'grace-gifts' should increase our understanding of what it means to 'grow in the *grace* and knowledge of our Lord and Saviour Jesus Christ'[1] and also that glorious statement of the Apostle John 'for of His fullness, we have all received and grace upon grace'.[2] We are not to become obsessed with knowing 'what my gift is'; rather, as we put down this book, we should turn afresh to the Grace-Giver, praying:

'Lord, I want to be a channel for your grace to be expressed in the congregation of your people. Lord, give more of Your fullness, grace upon grace and, within the spiritual body in which You have placed me, may I both receive grace through others and mediate grace to others, that there may be glory to You in the church and in Christ Jesus for ever and ever. Amen.'

'And since we have gifts (*charismata*, already possessed) that differ according to the grace given to us, let each exercise them accordingly: if prophecy according to the proportion of his faith; if service, in his serving; or he who teaches, in his teaching; or he who exhorts, in his exhortation; he who gives, with liberality; he who leads, with diligence; he who shows mercy, with cheerfulness. Let love be without hypocrisy.'[3]

[1] 2 Peter 3.18   [2] John 1.16   [3] Rom. 12.6-8

For further reading

BARCLAY, William. *New Testament Words*. Philadelphia: Westminster, 1976.

BARRETT, C. K. *First Epistle to the Corinthians*. New York: Harper & Row, 1968.

BITTLINGER, A. *Gifts and Graces*. Grand Rapids: Eerdmans, 1968.

BRIDGE, D. and PHYPERS, D. *Spiritual Gifts and the Church*. Downers Grove: Inter-Varsity, 1973.

BRUCE, F. F. *Corinthians, One and Two*. Greenwood, SC: Attic Press, 1971.

CLARK, Stephen B. *Spiritual Gifts*. Pecos, NM: Dove, 1969.

CROWE, P., HENDERSON, A. R., and PACKER, J. I. *Ministry in the Local Church*. (Grove Booklets No. 2) Bramcote Notts, 1972.

ELLIS, Earle. "The Role of the Christian Prophet in Acts," in Gasque and Martin, eds., *Apostolic History and the Gospel*. Grand Rapids: Eerdmans, 1970.

GOLDINGAY, John. *The Church and the Gifts of the Spirit*. (Grove Booklets No. 7) Bramcote Notts, 1972.

GREEN, Michael. *I Believe in the Holy Spirit*. Grand Rapids: Eerdmans, 1975.

MORRIS, Leon. *The First Epistle of Paul to the Corinthians*. Grand Rapids: Eerdmans, 1958.

MORRIS, Leon. *Ministers of God*. London: Inter-Varsity, 1964.

ROBERTSON, O. Palmer. "Tongues: Sign of Covenantal Curse and Blessing." *Westminster Theological Journal*.

STOTT, John R. W. *Baptism and Fullness*. Downers Grove: Inter-Varsity, 1976.

STOTT, John R. W. *The Preacher's Portrait in the New Testament*. Grand Rapids: Eerdmans, 1964.

WATSON, David. *One in the Spirit*. London: Hodder & Stoughton, 1973.